ELEVATE

UNDER PRESSURE

The Pressure Performance System
for Leaders Who Refuse to Break

SCOTT SADLER

ELEVATE UNDER PRESSURE™

The Pressure Performance System for Leaders Who Refuse to Break

For permission requests, contact the author at scott@scottsadlercoaching.com.

First edition, 2026

Published in the United States of America

ISBN (paperback): 979-8-9955439-0-9
ISBN (ebook): 979-8-9955439-1-6
ISBN (audiobook): 979-8-9955439-2-3

10 9 8 7 6 5 4 3 2 1

Cover design and interior layout by the author.

Disclaimer

The information contained in this book is provided for educational and informational purposes only. It is not intended as professional, legal, financial, medical, or psychological advice.

While the author draws on extensive experience in leadership, coaching, and human performance, the content is not a substitute for working directly with a qualified professional in any specific field.

Readers are encouraged to use their own judgment and seek appropriate professional guidance when making decisions that may impact their personal, professional, or organizational outcomes.

The author makes no guarantees regarding results, as outcomes will vary based on individual circumstances, application, and external factors.

By reading this book, you acknowledge that you are responsible for your own decisions, actions, and results.

scottsadlercoaching.com • elevateunderpressure.com

Dedication

For those who have stood in the pressure with me — clients, colleagues, mentors, coaches, and the people closest to home. You know who you are. This book is the proof of what you gave me.

CONTENTS

FOREWORD

To those lifelong learners.

Having recently retired after a gratifying five-decade career in executive leadership with medium-to-large corporations, I've had the privilege of collaborating with many leaders. Most were extremely talented but with varying degrees of resilience under pressure. Those with tools to navigate pressure often achieved the desired outcomes; those who broke under it would have benefited immensely from the insights in this book.

My first encounter with Scott was personal, over thirty years ago, early in my mountaineering adventures. A mutual friend brought us together, and we quickly bonded over our shared passion for the mountains. It was then that I came to appreciate Scott's natural leadership abilities, knowledge of the outdoors, and coaching instincts.

Our climbing adventures spanned multiple decades while our professional pursuits took different paths. Scott honed his coaching acumen and built an extensive clientele while I remained in the corporate world across both publicly traded and privately held companies.

We all have pivotal moments where circumstances lead us into unknown territory with only a faint view of the path forward. Mine is deeply personal — the sudden death of my son. Even then, Scott's innate ability to recognize the pressure I was under and provide the coaching necessary for me to heal and move forward was invaluable.

Scott's approach to leadership closely mirrors his approach to life, be straightforward, keep it genuine, be prepared, keep growing, and remain centered.

Early in our climbing days we would compare the weight of our packs — mine always weighed less, and I accused him of carrying unnecessary weight. On one climb, after my snide comment, Scott confidently replied, "There's nothing in my pack that you won't need." He was right. Shortly afterwards I discovered the going rate for toilet tissue that day was a dollar per sheet. Though he never charged me, it was one of many lessons from an admired coach, trusted advisor, and best of all, a lifelong friend.

Even the most accomplished C-Suite executives can fall to sustained pressure, failing to recognize when the water in the pot begins to boil. Emotional exhaustion and decision fatigue arrive first, followed by loss of credibility and eventual burnout — taking a toll on peers and results alike. None of us, regardless of talent or success, are immune to sustained pressure, but we can learn to harness it for improved performance.

This book takes a bold, forward-thinking look at managing that pressure by providing tools and systems for those willing to do the hard work. Given today's relentless pace, the constant flow of information, and emerging AI technologies, Elevate Under Pressure is an essential read for rising stars, executives, and decision-makers whose choices affect the people and organizations that trust them.

Mark Rosenfield VP of Retail Deli Sales, (Ret.) Reser's Fine Foods

---

PART ONE
THE PRESSURE REVEAL

INTRODUCTION PRESSURE DOESN'T REVEAL WEAKNESS. IT REVEALS IDENTITY.

"Most leaders don't fail because they lack skill. They fail because they lose access to it under pressure."

At fourteen years old, I got my first job in a small neighborhood restaurant. I was a dishwasher, a prep cook — whatever they needed. I was learning the rhythm of a kitchen, the pace of service, the unspoken rules of a team under pressure.

But it was at sixteen that everything changed.

That's when I stepped onto my first high-end restaurant line. Orders flying. Tickets stacking. Heat pouring from the pass and the ovens. Around me, seasoned professionals were moving at speeds I'd never seen — precision, recovery, split-second decisions, zero margin for error. You either had the tools or you didn't. You either found a way to perform or you got off the line.

I learned something in that kitchen that changed everything: pressure doesn't break you. It reveals you. And more importantly — it teaches you, if you're willing to learn.

That was forty years ago. Since then, I've stood in a lot of pressure moments.

I built and scaled a company from zero to 120 employees and $1.2 million in revenue. I navigated the dissolution of that business partnership — one of the hardest pressures any founder ever faces, and the one most business books skip right over because it's too human, too messy, too real. I grew a coaching practice over sixteen years, witnessing leadership and life growth in hundreds of people. I survived cancer, thanks to my barber. I served as a Chief People Officer, learning firsthand that the people side of leadership isn't a soft skill. It's the hardest skill. It's where organizations either elevate or collapse under pressure.

And through all of it, I kept testing pressure in every domain I could find — on mountains, in ultramarathons, through a massive personal betrayal in 2024 that demanded I still show up for my clients, for my work, for myself — under the full emotional weight of it.

And right now, in this season of my life, I am caring for my wife who has advanced Alzheimer's and for my mother at eighty-two. The pressure is relentless. It's intimate. It doesn't announce itself with a deadline or a board meeting. It just arrives every morning and asks the same quiet, unrelenting question: *Who are you going to be today?*

Skill gets you to the room. Identity decides what happens in it.

Here's What I've Discovered

The leaders who elevate under pressure aren't the ones who have less of it. They're not the ones with perfect circumstances, unlimited resources, or teams that never fail them. They're the ones who have learned something most people spend their whole careers — and their whole lives — avoiding.

They've learned to let pressure work for them.

Not by grinding harder. Not by building thicker skin or learning to "manage stress." Those ideas miss the point entirely. The real work is deeper — and more human. It's about understanding who you are when everything gets hard. It's about learning to regulate your nervous system so you think from your brain instead of your survival instincts. It's about building the execution discipline to act with clarity and intention, not adrenaline and reaction.

Over the past four decades, I've watched this pattern repeat across every high-pressure environment I've worked in — kitchens, startups, boardrooms, mountains, coaching sessions. The leaders who rise don't have a secret gene. They have a system, even if they've never named it.

I didn't invent it in a boardroom or a classroom. I discovered it on a kitchen line at sixteen. I tested it by building a business from nothing. I refined it by navigating a partnership that fell apart. I deepened it as a Chief People Officer watching culture bend and break under organizational pressure. And I've sharpened it through coaching hundreds of leaders, entrepreneurs, and high performers who all faced the same question: *How do I perform at my best when the pressure is at its worst?*

What This Book Is

This book is for leaders and entrepreneurs who operate in high-stakes environments. You're the ones who feel the weight. You're the ones making decisions that affect other people's livelihoods. You're the ones who can't afford to show up as anything less than your best — and you know the pressure is never going to stop coming.

You don't need another book about resilience. You need a system. You need tools. You need a fundamental shift in how you relate to pressure — from something you endure to something you use.

> **Identity Clarity** — understanding who you actually are under pressure, not who you think you should be. Most leaders have never asked this question clearly enough, and it costs them.
>
> **Emotional Regulation** — composure as a learned discipline, not a personality trait. The most composed leaders you've ever met weren't born that way. They built it.
>
> **Execution Discipline** — the systems and practices that let you perform consistently, not just when the adrenaline is pumping. Because adrenaline is not a strategy.

By the end of this book you'll have frameworks you can apply immediately. You'll have real stories — from my life, from my clients, from leaders who faced impossible pressure and found a way through it. And you'll have shifted something fundamental about how you see pressure itself.

The only question that matters is: Who will you be when you do?

The Real Question

There's a personal invitation here that I want to be direct about.

Pressure will always be part of your life. If you're a leader, if you're building something, if you care deeply about people and outcomes — pressure is the price of entry. The question has never been whether you'll face it. The only question that matters is: *Who will you be when you do?*

That's what this book is really about. Not escaping pressure. Not managing it. Not white-knuckling through it until it passes. But elevating through it — becoming the version of yourself that pressure has always been trying to teach you to become.

Pressure doesn't reveal weakness. It reveals identity.

And the leaders who elevate under pressure aren't the ones who have less of it. They're the ones who have learned to let it work for them.

That person isn't someone else.

That's you.

You just need the system.

Let's begin.

1

PRESSURE DOESN'T BREAK LEADERS. IT REVEALS THEM.

There's a moment every leader knows.

It doesn't announce itself. It doesn't give you time to prepare. It just arrives — a phone call, a number on a spreadsheet, a conversation that goes sideways, a team member who quits at the worst possible moment, a market shift that changes everything overnight.

And in that moment, before you've had time to think, before you've had time to strategize or consult or breathe — you react.

That reaction? That's not showing your weakness. That's not your inexperience or your inadequacy. That's your identity showing. Who you've been trained to be. Who you've decided to become. The stories you've told yourself about pressure, performance, and what it means to lead.

And here's the truth most leadership books won't tell you: most leaders have never examined that identity. They've never looked at how they default under pressure and asked: *Is this who I want to be? Or is this just who I've become by accident?*

That's what this chapter is about.

The Myth of the Pressure-Proof Leader

We have a story in our culture about great leaders. They're calm. They're decisive. They never panic. They walk into a burning room and somehow lower the temperature just by being there.

We call it "grace under pressure." We treat it like a personality trait — something you either have or you don't. Either you're built for pressure or you're not. Either you thrive under heat or you wilt.

That story is a lie.

I've coached hundreds of leaders — executives, entrepreneurs, founders, scaling companies, Chief Executive Officers rebuilding culture from the inside out. I've never met one who was born performing well under pressure. Not one. What I have met — every single time — are leaders who learned how to perform under pressure. Who built the identity and the tools and the disciplines that let them show up clearly and decisively when the heat came.

The difference between a leader who elevates under pressure and one who collapses isn't personality. It isn't talent. It isn't even experience.

It's identity clarity. And it's learnable.

Pressure is not a test you pass or fail. It's a mirror that shows you who you are.

What Pressure Actually Does

Let me tell you what pressure actually does to the human system — because understanding this changes everything.

When pressure hits, your brain registers a threat. Your nervous system activates. Cortisol and adrenaline flood your body. Your prefrontal cortex — the part of your brain responsible for clear thinking, strategic decision-making, and emotional regulation — starts to go offline. And your survival brain — the part that's been keeping humans alive for hundreds of thousands of years — takes over.

This is not a weakness. This is biology. This is your system doing exactly what it was designed to do.

The problem is that the survival brain is not equipped to lead a company, manage a team, or navigate a high-stakes negotiation. It's equipped to fight, flee, or freeze. And when leaders are operating from a survival brain — even leaders who look calm on the outside — their decisions suffer. Their communication suffers. Their relationships suffer. And over time, their performance suffers.

The leaders who elevate under pressure have learned one critical skill above all others: they've learned to recognize when their survival brain is driving, and they've built the tools to bring their thinking brain back online — fast, consistently, and under any conditions.

That's *Emotional Regulation*. We'll go deep on that in Chapter 5. But first, we need to understand something even more foundational: what pressure reveals about who you think you are.

The Identity Reveal

I want to tell you about two leaders I've worked with at two different companies. Marcus and Diana, not their real names.

Marcus is a founder. Built a technology company from zero, scaled it to forty employees, raised a significant round of funding. By every external measure, he was crushing it. Until the day a key client representing thirty percent of his revenue sent him an email saying they were moving to a competitor.

In that moment — before he called his team, before he consulted his CFO, before he did anything strategic — Marcus did something he'd done his whole career. He fixed it. Alone. He stayed up all night building a proposal to win the client back. He micromanaged his account team. He made promises he wasn't sure he could keep. He bypassed his own leadership team and went directly to the client contact.

The client left anyway. And Marcus spent the next three months rebuilding trust with a team that felt bypassed and undervalued.

When Marcus and I unpacked that moment in our coaching, we found something he'd never examined: Marcus had a deeply held belief that he was the solution to every crisis. That his value as a leader was in fixing things — fast, alone, brilliantly. That belief served him when he was a solo founder. It became a liability when he was leading a team.

Pressure didn't create that pattern. It revealed it.

Diana is a Chief Operating Officer at a mid-size healthcare organization. Brilliant, strategic, respected. But when budget season came — when the pressure of competing priorities and limited resources and executive conflict hit its peak — Diana went quiet. She stopped advocating for her team. She deferred to more aggressive voices in the room even when she knew they were wrong. She told herself she was being strategic. Her team experienced it as abandonment.

When we explored this together, Diana found something she'd carried since childhood: a belief that conflict meant danger. That keeping the peace was safer than speaking up. Pressure didn't create that belief. It revealed it.

Marcus and Diana both had real capability. Both had real leadership instincts. But under pressure, they both defaulted to an identity that wasn't serving them — and they'd never examined it because pressure had never held up a mirror long enough for them to look.

Your pressure default is not your destiny.

Pressure Is a Mirror

Here's the reframe I want you to carry through this entire book:

Pressure is not a test you pass or fail. It's a mirror that shows you who you are.

And here's the radical part: that mirror is a gift. Because you cannot change what you cannot see. And pressure — as uncomfortable as it is — shows you exactly what needs to change.

The leaders who elevate under pressure aren't the ones who have figured out how to avoid the mirror. They're the ones who have learned to look into it — clearly, honestly, without flinching — and use what they see to become better.

That's the foundation of the Pressure Performance System. Not fixing your weaknesses. Not grinding harder. But seeing yourself clearly under pressure and making a conscious choice about who you want to be.

Your Pressure Default

Every leader has a pressure default. A pattern they fall into when the heat comes — before they've had time to think, before they've chosen. It's the response that's been rehearsed so many times it feels automatic.

Some leaders become Fixers — like Marcus. They take over, micromanage, solve alone, bypass their teams. They're driven by a deep belief that their value is in having the answer.

Some leaders become Peacekeepers — like Diana. They go quiet, defer, avoid conflict. They're driven by a belief that keeping the peace is safer than speaking the truth.

Some leaders become Performers — high energy, high visibility, filling the room with confidence even when they're terrified inside. Driven by a belief that they must always appear capable.

Some leaders become Withdrawers — they disappear into data, analysis, planning. Anything to avoid the human mess of pressure. Driven by a belief that if they just get the numbers right, everything will be okay.

None of these defaults are wrong. All of them were adaptive at some point — they helped you survive something. But under sustained pressure, in high-stakes leadership environments, they all have a cost.

In Chapter 3, we'll go deep on identifying your specific pressure profile. But for now, I want you to sit with one question:

When pressure hits — before you think, before you choose — what do you do?

That answer is your starting point. And it's more valuable than anything else in this book.

The Good News

Here's what forty years of living and working under pressure has taught me:

Your pressure default is not your destiny.

The pattern you fall into when the heat comes — the identity that pressure reveals — is not fixed. It's not who you are forever. It's who you've become through a combination of experience, belief, and habit. And all of those things can change.

That's what The Pressure Performance System is designed to do. Not to make you someone different. To make you someone more — more clear, more regulated, more disciplined. More fully yourself, with intention, under any conditions.

The kitchen at sixteen taught me that. Five hundred dinners a night, guests watching, tickets flying — you don't survive that by accident. You survive it by building something inside yourself that pressure can't touch. An identity that holds. A set of tools that work. A clarity about who you are and how you perform that no amount of heat can shake.

That's what we're building in this book. Together.

At the end of each chapter, you'll find a Pressure Reflection — a short set of questions designed to help you apply what you've just read to your own leadership reality. Don't skip these. The insight is in the reflection.

Pressure Reflection: Chapter 1

Before you move into the next chapter — where we go deeper into what happens inside leaders when pressure hits — I want you to do something most leaders never take time to do: sit with what pressure has already been trying to tell you.

This isn't an assessment. It's an honest conversation with yourself.

Step One:

Think about your last significant pressure moment. Not a minor inconvenience — a real one. A decision that kept you up at night. A relationship that fractured under stress. A season where you wondered if you had what it took. Write it down in one or two sentences. Just name it.

Step Two:

Ask the revealing question. At that moment, what did pressure expose about you? Not what you did wrong — what it revealed. Did it show you that you default to control when you're afraid? That you go quiet when you should speak? That you push people away when you need them most? That you perform brilliantly under external pressure but collapse under internal pressure? Don't judge it. Just name it.

Step Three:

Separate the story from the truth. Most leaders carry a story about their pressure moment — *I failed. I wasn't ready. I should have known better.* Underneath that story is usually a truth that's more useful. Write down the story you've been telling yourself. Then write down what the pressure actually revealed — the identity underneath the event.

Step Four:

Ask the forward question. If pressure reveals identity, and you now know what it's been revealing about you — who do you want it to reveal going forward? Not a perfect version of yourself. The next version. The leader who's one degree more regulated, one degree more clear, one degree more intentional under heat.

Write that person down. That's who this book is for.

2
THE ALIGNMENT GAP — WHY PRESSURE BREAKS MOST LEADERS

There's a story I hear constantly in my work with executives and entrepreneurs. It goes something like this:

"I've handled pressure my whole career. I don't know why this time feels different."

And when I sit with that statement long enough — when we slow it down and look at what's actually happening — the answer is almost never what they expect. It's not that the pressure got bigger. It's not that they got weaker. It's that somewhere along the way, the pressure pulled them out of alignment with who they are, and they've been performing from that fractured place ever since.

That's the real problem. Not pressure. Misalignment.

Misalignment under pressure is the most expensive leadership problem in business today.

What Misalignment Actually Looks Like

Misalignment doesn't announce itself. It doesn't show up as a crisis moment where everything falls apart at once. It shows up quietly — in the patterns leaders develop under pressure when they don't have a system to stay grounded.

It looks like the CEO who can't make a clear decision because she's managing everyone else's reactions to the decision instead of leading from her own clarity.

It looks like the founder who avoids the tough conversation with his senior leader for six months because the emotional cost feels too high — while his best people watch and quietly update their resumes.

It looks like the executive who walks into a high-stakes negotiation fully prepared on paper, but unregulated emotionally — and concedes too early because the other side pushed a button he didn't know he had.

It looks like the leader who starts micromanaging when revenue slips — adding meetings, demanding more reports, tightening control — while the very team he needs to perform begins to disengage.

None of these leaders are weak. None of them are incompetent. They're misaligned. And misalignment under pressure is the most expensive leadership problem in business today.

The Five Pressure Arenas Where Misalignment Breaks Leaders

In my work with executives across industries, I've identified five core arenas where pressure fractures leadership most consistently. These aren't abstract concepts — they're the specific situations your team is navigating right now.

Decision Pressure — When you must make high-impact decisions with incomplete data. Strategic pivots. Crisis response. Budget tradeoffs with no good options. The misaligned leader makes these decisions from fear, political calculation, or emotional bias. The aligned leader makes them from a place of clarity.

Conflict Pressure — When human tension threatens to derail performance. Executive team disagreements. Culture clashes. The tough performance conversation that keeps getting postponed. The misaligned leader avoids or escalates. The aligned leader names the real issue and leads through it.

Negotiation Pressure — Where stakes, ego, and economics collide. Enterprise deals. Partnership renewals. Compensation discussions. The misaligned leader loses emotional leverage and signals weakness at the critical moment. The aligned leader regulates first, then leads the room.

Change Pressure — Where organizations must move faster than their comfort level. Restructures. Transformations. Layoffs. The misaligned leader manages optics instead of leading change. The aligned leader connects the why to the daily execution and equips their next layer to carry it forward.

Performance Pressure — Where leaders must deliver results through people who are stretched. Revenue targets. Succession gaps. High-performer burnout. The misaligned leader becomes the bottleneck. The aligned leader multiplies capacity.

Here's what all five of these arenas have in common: they don't break organizations. Unregulated, misaligned leaders do.

The Eight Moments Where Misalignment Costs You Everything

Within those five arenas, there are eight specific moments where misalignment breaks leadership most often. You'll recognize these. You may have lived some of them.

The high-stakes call with incomplete data.

The board wants an answer by Friday. The data is 60% there. The team is split. The leader who hesitates loses credibility. The leader who rushes loses trust. This is where emotional bias overrides strategic clarity — and careers get defined by a single quarter.

The leadership team that won't align.

Three VPs. Three agendas. One strategy meeting that ends in polite silence and passive resistance. This is not a strategy problem. It's an identity conflict disguised as a business disagreement. Everyone is protecting their own territory because pressure has made them self-preserving instead of mission-driven.

The tough conversation that keeps getting postponed.

A senior leader is underperforming. Everyone sees it. No one says it. Weeks become months. The team's respect erodes quietly. What looks like loyalty is actually fear — and the cost is invisible until it isn't.

The negotiation where leverage disappears.

The executive walks in prepared on paper but unregulated emotionally. They concede too early, get reactive to a provocation, or lose composure when the other side pushes back. The real loss isn't the deal terms — it's the signal they send about who they are under pressure.

Change doesn't break organizations. Unregulated leaders do.

The transformation that stalls at the middle.

The restructure was announced. The vision was clear at the top. But six months in, execution has flatlined. Middle management is frozen, waiting for someone above them to go first. The senior leader starts managing optics instead of leading change.

The quarter where the numbers are slipping.

Revenue is down. The leader starts micromanaging. More meetings. More reports. Tighter control. Which signals panic to the very people who need to feel steady — and kills the initiative the team needs most.

The succession gap no one is naming.

The top leader is carrying everything. Below them, no one is ready. Not because the talent isn't there, but because no one has been developed to lead under pressure. The organization has built executors, not leaders.

The public moment that exposes the leader.

The all-hands after a crisis. The town hall where employees are angry. The board meeting where the numbers didn't land. The whole organization is watching to see who their leader really is. And pressure doesn't build character in public — it reveals it.

Why Misalignment Happens

Here's the core truth that most leadership frameworks miss: when pressure rises, identity drives behavior.

Not strategy. Not training. Not tenure. Identity.

When you don't have clarity about who you are under pressure — your values, your defaults, your patterns — pressure will make that decision for you. And it will almost always pull you toward survival behavior: self-protection, control, avoidance, or reaction.

This is not a character flaw. It's neuroscience. When the brain perceives a threat, it moves toward survival mode. The prefrontal cortex — your thinking brain, your strategic brain, the part of you that leads with wisdom — starts to go offline. The amygdala takes over. And the amygdala is excellent at keeping you alive. It is terrible at leading a team through a transformation, having a courageous conversation, or making a clear decision in a board meeting.

The leaders who elevate under pressure aren't the ones who don't feel that pull toward survival. They feel it. They've just learned something that changes everything: you can regulate your nervous system, return to your thinking brain, and lead from alignment — even when everything is on the line.

That's not a gift. It's a skill. And it's exactly what the Pressure Performance System is designed to build.

The Alignment Gap

I want you to think about the last time you felt truly clear under pressure. Decisive. Grounded. Present. Leading from your best self instead of your most defended self.

Now think about the last time pressure pulled you somewhere you didn't want to go. Reactive. Avoidant. Controlling. Performing instead of leading.

The distance between those two experiences is what I call the Alignment Gap. And every leader has one. The question is whether you have a system to close it — or whether you're leaving it to chance every time the heat rises.

Most leaders are leaving it to chance. They've never been given a framework for understanding their pressure defaults. They've never learned to regulate their nervous system as a leadership discipline. They've never built the execution systems that let them perform consistently instead of reactively.

The Pressure Performance System closes that gap. It doesn't eliminate pressure — nothing does, nothing should. It gives you the tools to stay aligned inside the pressure, so that who you are under heat is the same person you are when everything is calm.

What Alignment Actually Produces

When leaders close the Alignment Gap, something shifts — not just in their performance, but in everything around them.

Decisions get made faster and with more conviction. Not because the data improved, but because the leader is no longer paralyzed by the emotional weight of the decision.

Tough conversations get had. Not because conflict suddenly feels comfortable, but because the leader has the internal regulation to hold the discomfort and lead through it anyway.

Teams perform better. Not because the leader got tougher, but because regulated leaders create psychological safety — and psychological safety is where discretionary effort lives.

Culture strengthens. Not because of a new values initiative, but because the leader's behavior under pressure became the culture.

This is what alignment produces. And this is what the Pressure Performance System is designed to deliver.

In the next chapter, we're going to get specific about you — how you personally default under pressure, what your Pressure Profile looks like, and how to use that self-knowledge as the foundation for everything that follows.

Because before you can close the Alignment Gap, you have to understand where you are starting from.

"Misalignment under pressure is the most expensive leadership problem in business today."

— *Elevate Under Pressure*, Chapter 2

3
THE PRESSURE MAP — FIVE ARENAS AND EIGHT PRESSURE POINTS

In the last chapter, we named the real problem: misalignment. We explored the Alignment Gap — the distance between who you are under pressure and who you want to be. And we saw that when leaders don't have a system for staying grounded under heat, pressure doesn't break the organization. The leader's unregulated response does.

Now I want to get specific. Because misalignment doesn't happen in the abstract. It happens in specific, recurring situations that every executive faces. The same arenas, the same pressure points, the same fracture patterns — playing out across industries, company sizes, and leadership levels.

What I'm about to show you is the landscape of executive pressure. Not theory. The actual terrain your leadership operates in every day. These are the arenas where performance risk is highest. And inside those arenas, the eight specific moments where pressure breaks leadership most often.

This is the leadership capability required when performance risk is highest.

The Five Core Enterprise Pressure Arenas

In my work with executives across industries — from $20 million mid-market companies to billion-dollar enterprises — I've identified five core arenas where pressure fractures leadership most consistently. These aren't categories I invented in a strategy session. They emerged from hundreds of coaching engagements, leadership team interventions, and the lived experience of building and leading organizations under real conditions.

Every executive operates in all five. But most leaders have one or two arenas where their nervous system fires hardest and their defaults show up fastest. Knowing which arenas are yours is foundational to everything that follows.

1. Decision Pressure

When leaders must make high-impact decisions with incomplete data.

> Where it shows up: Strategic pivots. Mergers and acquisitions. Market disruption. Crisis response. Budget tradeoffs with no good options.
>
> What executives fear: Poor judgment under pressure. Emotional bias. Political decision-making that protects careers instead of building the organization.
>
> The truth: The leaders who win are not the calmest. They are the most aligned under pressure. A regulated leader with sixty percent of the data will outperform a dysregulated leader with ninety percent, every time.

2. Conflict Pressure

When leaders must manage human tension without losing performance.

Where it shows up: Executive team disagreements. Cross-functional conflict. Culture clashes. Leadership misalignment. The tough performance conversation that keeps getting postponed.

What executives fear: Conflict avoidance that masquerades as diplomacy. Emotional reactions that fracture trust. Loss of alignment in the leadership team that cascades through the organization.

The truth: When pressure rises, identity drives behavior. Aligned leaders don't become the pressure they're trying to manage. They regulate first, name the real issue, and lead through it.

3. Negotiation Pressure

Where stakes, ego, and economics collide.

Where it shows up: Enterprise sales. Strategic partnerships. Vendor negotiations. Labor discussions. Compensation conversations. Acquisitions.

What executives fear: Losing emotional leverage at the critical moment. Reactive decision-making driven by the other side's tactics. Conceding too early because the discomfort of holding position feels too high.

The truth: Pressure exposes identity. Leaders who regulate themselves control the negotiation. Leaders who don't, signal to the other side exactly where they'll fold.

4. Change Pressure

Where organizations must move faster than their comfort level.

Where it shows up: Transformation initiatives. Restructures. Digital change. Culture shifts. Layoffs. Leadership transitions.

What executives fear: Resistance that stalls execution. Leadership misalignment between the pace the board wants and the pace the organization can absorb. Burnout and disengagement in the people carrying the change.

The truth: Change doesn't break organizations. Unregulated leaders do. The leader who manages optics instead of leading change creates the very resistance they're afraid of.

5. Performance Pressure

Where leaders must deliver results through people who are stretched.

Where it shows up: Revenue targets. Succession gaps. High-performer burnout. Accountability gaps. Bench strength that can't hold the weight.

What executives fear: Talent collapse under sustained pressure. Leadership bottlenecks where one person is carrying everything. Weak bench strength that leaves the organization one departure away from crisis.

The truth: Pressure reveals leadership capacity. The Pressure Performance System multiplies it. The goal is not a leader who performs harder — it's a system that develops the next layer to lead under pressure, not just execute tasks.

These five arenas are where your leadership is tested most consistently. And here's what they all have in common: the pressure in each arena is not the problem. The problem is what the pressure reveals about the leader's alignment — their clarity, their regulation, their execution discipline. Fix the leader's alignment, and the arena becomes manageable. Leave the leader misaligned, and the arena becomes a recurring fracture that no strategy, no hire, and no restructure can solve.

The leaders who win are not the calmest. They are the most aligned under pressure.

The Eight Executive Pressure Points

Inside those five arenas, there are eight specific, recurring moments where pressure breaks leadership most often. These aren't hypothetical. They're the exact situations I encounter in my coaching work week after week. You'll recognize them. You've probably lived several of them this quarter.

Each pressure point cuts across one or more arenas. Each one creates a leadership fracture that cascades through teams, culture, and results. And each one is solvable — not by removing the pressure, but by building the internal capacity to lead through it.

1. The High-Stakes Call With Incomplete Data

The board wants an answer by Friday. The data is sixty percent there. The team is split. The leader who hesitates loses credibility. The leader who rushes loses trust. This is where emotional bias overrides strategic clarity — and careers get defined by a single quarter.

Arena: Decision Pressure

What the system solves: Regulate first — bring the thinking brain online before the survival brain makes the call. Reframe the decision from survival to strategy. Decide from clarity and values, not from fear of how the board will react.

2. The Leadership Team That Won't Align

Three VPs. Three agendas. One strategy meeting that ends in polite silence and passive resistance. This is not a strategy problem. It's an identity conflict disguised as a business disagreement. Everyone is protecting their own territory because pressure has made them self-preserving instead of mission-driven.

Arena: Conflict Pressure

What the system solves: Identity Clarity exposes the real conflict underneath the polite disagreement. Emotional Regulation breaks the reactive loops that keep the team stuck. When each leader can regulate their own nervous system and reframe the conflict as a challenge instead of a threat, alignment becomes possible — not forced compliance, but genuine shared commitment.

3. The Tough Conversation That Keeps Getting Postponed

A senior leader is underperforming. Everyone sees it. No one says it. Weeks become months. The team's respect erodes quietly. What looks like loyalty is actually fear — fear of conflict, fear of the other person's reaction, fear of being the one who made it real.

Arena: Conflict Pressure + Performance Pressure

What the system solves: Emotional Regulation creates the internal safety to have the conversation — not when it's comfortable, but when it's needed. Execution Discipline turns it into a clear, scheduled, non-negotiable action. The Pressure Performance System doesn't make the conversation easy. It makes it possible.

4. The Negotiation Where Leverage Disappears

A critical deal. A partnership renewal. A board compensation discussion. The executive walks in prepared on paper but unregulated emotionally. They concede too early, get reactive to a provocation, or lose composure when the other side pushes back. The real loss isn't the deal terms — it's the signal they send about who they are under pressure.

Arena: Negotiation Pressure

What the system solves: Regulate the nervous system before you enter the room. Reframe the pressure from threat to fuel. Leaders who regulate themselves control the negotiation. Leaders who don't, signal exactly where the other side should push.

5. The Transformation That Stalls at the Middle

The restructure was announced. The vision was clear at the top. But six months in, execution has flatlined. Middle management is frozen — overwhelmed, under-resourced, and waiting for someone above them to go first. The senior leader is caught between the board's timeline and the organization's emotional capacity. They start managing optics instead of leading change.

Arena: Change Pressure

What the system solves: Execution Discipline reconnects the daily work to the strategic why. The system equips the next layer of leaders to carry the change forward instead of waiting for permission. Regulate, Reframe, Decide, Execute — applied at every layer, not just the top.

6. The Quarter Where the Numbers Are Slipping

Revenue is down. The pipeline is thin. The team is grinding but results aren't materializing. The leader starts micromanaging — adding meetings, demanding more reports, tightening control — which signals panic to the very people who need to feel steady. The harder they grip, the more talent disengages.

Arena: Performance Pressure

What the system solves: Execution Discipline replaces panic with process. Emotional Regulation prevents the leader from becoming the source of the team's stress. Reframe the pressure from threat to challenge — because a team led by a regulated leader who sees a challenge will outperform a team led by a dysregulated leader who sees a crisis.

7. The Succession Gap No One Is Naming

The top leader is carrying everything. Below them, no one is ready. The bench is thin — not because the talent isn't there, but because no one has been developed to lead under pressure. They've been managed, not multiplied. The organization has built executors, not leaders. When the senior person exits, burns out, or gets promoted, the whole system wobbles.

Arena: Performance Pressure + Change Pressure

What the system solves: The Pressure Performance System isn't just for the leader at the top. It's designed to be transmitted to the next layer — building leaders who can regulate, reframe, decide, and execute under pressure independently. This is the only sustainable growth strategy: developing the capacity to lead under heat at every level, not just concentrating it in one person.

8. The Public Moment That Exposes the Leader

The all-hands meeting after a crisis. The earnings call didn't go well. The town hall where employees are angry and asking hard questions. The whole organization is watching to see who their leader really is. The executive who is unregulated gets defensive. The executive who lacks identity clarity reads from a script and loses the room. Pressure doesn't build character in public — it reveals it.

Arena: All five — Decision, Conflict, Negotiation, Change, and Performance converge in a single moment

What the system solves: This is the moment where the full Pressure Performance System earns its place. Regulate first — because a dysregulated leader in a public moment doesn't just lose the room, they become the story. Reframe the moment from threat to opportunity: this isn't an interrogation, it's the most visible leadership moment of the year, and the organization will remember who showed up. Decide from identity and values, not from the impulse to defend or perform — what the room needs is not a polished answer, it's a leader who is grounded enough to tell the truth and steady enough to hold the discomfort. Execute with discipline in the follow-through, because the public moment doesn't end when the meeting ends. It ends when the team sees that what the leader said in public is what the leader does in the weeks that follow.

Pressure doesn't build character in public — it reveals it.

Finding Yourself in the Landscape

Here's why this chapter matters for what comes next.

In the next chapter, we're going to build your Pressure Profile — the specific combination of defaults, arenas, and identity triggers that define how you personally respond under heat. That profile is your starting point for the Pressure Performance System. And the more precisely you understand the landscape you're operating in, the more precisely the system can work for you.

Most leadership development is generic. It teaches broad principles and hopes they apply when the pressure arrives. The Pressure Performance System is specific. It's designed for the five arenas you just read about and the eight pressure points that live *inside* them. It's designed for the moments where leadership actually happens — not the moments where it's easy.

Before you move to the next chapter, I want you to sit with two questions.

First: Which of the five arenas triggers your defaults hardest? Not all pressure is the same for every leader. Some leaders are steady under decision pressure but fracture under conflict pressure. Some leaders thrive in negotiation but collapse under change pressure. Your arena tells you where your nervous system is most vulnerable — and where the Pressure Performance System will give you the most immediate return.

Second: Which of the eight pressure points are you living right now? Not last year. Right now. Which one is costing you sleep, credibility, relationships, or results this quarter? Name it. That's not just diagnostic. That's your training ground for everything in Part Two.

Pressure Reflection: Chapter 3

These questions connect the landscape to your leadership reality.

Question One:

Rank the five pressure arenas from the one that triggers your defaults most to the one where you're most steady: Decision, Conflict, Negotiation, Change, Performance. Don't overthink it. Your nervous system already knows the order. Trust the first answer that comes.

Question Two:

Of the eight pressure points, which one are you facing right now? Which one has been recurring in your leadership over the past twelve months? If more than one applies, name the one that's costing you the most — in credibility, relationships, results, or your own well-being.

Question Three:

For the pressure point you named, identify the arena it lives in. Then ask: is that the same arena where your defaults fire hardest? If the answer is yes, you've found the intersection where the Pressure Performance System will make the biggest immediate difference in your leadership.

Question Four:

Think about the last time you were inside one of the eight pressure points and your leadership fractured — even slightly. What happened? What did you do? And if you could go back to that moment with the ability to Regulate, Reframe, Decide, and Execute in sequence, what would have been different? Hold that image. You're about to build the capacity to make it real.

Question Five:

Look at the five arenas again. Which one does your organization struggle with most? Not you personally — your team, your leadership layer, your company. The arena that's weakest in your organization is likely the one where unregulated leadership defaults have been cascading the longest. That's the systemic problem. And it's the one that Part Three of this book will address.

In the next chapter, we go personal. Your Pressure Profile — the specific defaults, arenas, and identity triggers that define how you show up under heat — is the foundation for everything in the Pressure Performance System. The landscape is now clear. It's time to find where you stand in it.

> *"Exceptional leadership capability is required when performance risk is highest."*
>
> **— *Elevate Under Pressure*, Chapter 3**

4

YOUR PRESSURE PROFILE — HOW YOU DEFAULT UNDER HEAT

There's a moment every leader knows.

The meeting shifts. The numbers come in wrong. The phone rings at the worst possible time. A key person resigns. A deal falls apart. A partner betrays you.

And in that split second — before you say a word, before you make a single decision — something happens inside you. Your nervous system fires. Your identity kicks in. And you default.

The question isn't whether you default under pressure. Every leader does. The question is: *what do you default to?*

Because here's what I've learned coaching executives and entrepreneurs through every kind of high-stakes moment: most leaders have never actually studied their own pressure response. They've survived it. They've pushed through it. They've even learned to function in spite of it. But they've never stopped to ask the most important diagnostic question in leadership development:

Who am I when the heat comes?

That's what this chapter is designed to help you discover.

Your Default Response: The Four Patterns

When pressure hits one of these eight moments, leaders don't respond randomly. They default to one of four primary patterns. Understanding yours is the foundation of everything that follows in this book.

The Controller tightens their grip. More meetings. More oversight. More checking in. They believe that if they can just manage the variables closely enough, they can contain the pressure. What they're actually doing is signaling panic to their team and eliminating the autonomy their people need to perform.

The Avoider postpones. The tough conversation gets delayed another week. The underperforming leader gets another quarter. The decision gets tabled pending more data. Avoidance feels like wisdom — like patience or strategy — but it's almost always fear wearing a professional mask.

The Reactor responds from emotion before they respond from thought. They go sharp in meetings. They send emails they regret. They make decisions from the survival brain instead of the thinking brain. Speed feels like decisiveness, but reaction without regulation is just chaos with authority.

The Disconnector goes quiet. Withdraws from the team. Stops communicating. Becomes unreadable. Their silence creates a vacuum that the team fills with anxiety, speculation, and worst-case assumptions. Disconnection feels like composure from the inside. From the outside it looks like abandonment.

None of these patterns are character flaws. They are nervous system responses — strategies that worked at some point in your life or career and got wired in as your automatic answer to pressure. The problem isn't that you have a default. The problem is operating from it unconsciously, without the awareness or tools to choose differently.

That's what the Pressure Performance System gives you: the awareness to see your default clearly, and the system to override it with intention.

The pattern is not the prison. The pattern is just the door you walk through when the pressure comes.

The Pressure Performance Response

When pressure rises, the Pressure Performance System activates through four sequential moves. Regulate — name it, slow it, choose your state before you choose your response. Reframe — reinterpret the situation, shift from threat to challenge, lead the narrative. Decide — clarify the decision, align it to identity and values, move with conviction rather than reaction. Execute — follow through with discipline, protect standards, deliver under fire.

This isn't a theory. It's a real-time protocol that rewires how you respond to pressure at the moment it matters most. And it starts with the first move — Regulate — because without that, none of the others are possible.

You cannot reframe clearly from a survival brain. You cannot decide wisely from panic. You cannot execute with discipline from adrenaline.

Regulation is the master skill. It's the one that makes all the others accessible.

Discovering Your Pressure Profile

Most leaders don't discover their pressure profile in a coaching session or a workshop. They discover it in a moment they'd rather forget.

It's the meeting where they said something sharp and watched the room go quiet. The quarter where they micromanaged their best people into disengagement. The relationship that fractured because they went silent when they should have spoken. The decision they delayed so long it made the choice for them.

Those moments aren't failures. They're data. And when you learn to read that data clearly — without shame, without defense, without the story that you should have known better — they become the most valuable leadership intelligence you have.

Your pressure profile is built from three layers. The first is your dominant default pattern — Controller, Avoider, Reactor, or Disconnector. The second is your primary pressure arena — the specific domain where your default fires hardest and fastest. The third is your identity trigger — the core belief underneath the pattern that pressure activates before you've had time to think.

Most leadership development works on the behavior. The Pressure Performance System works on all three layers — because behavior change without identity work doesn't hold under heat. You can learn a new communication technique in a training room and completely forget it the moment your CFO tells you revenue is down thirty percent.

Real change under pressure requires going deeper. It requires understanding not just what you do, but *why* — and whether that why still serves you.

The Identity Trigger Underneath Your Default

Every pressure default has a root. A belief that got installed early — in a family system, a formative experience, a season of your career where a particular response kept you safe or helped you succeed.

The Controller often carries a belief that sounds like: *If I don't manage this, it falls apart. My value is in having the answer.* This belief may have been forged in a childhood where things actually did fall apart when no one was in charge. Or in an early career win that came entirely from personal heroics. It served a purpose. Under sustained leadership pressure, it becomes a liability.

The Avoider often carries a belief that sounds like: *Conflict means danger. Keeping the peace is safer than speaking the truth.* This belief may have come from a volatile environment where conflict had real consequences. The nervous system learned: don't escalate, don't provoke, wait it out. In a kitchen at sixteen, that might have been wisdom. In a boardroom at fifty, it's costing you.

The Reactor often carries a belief that sounds like: *Speed is strength. Decisiveness is leadership. Hesitation means weakness.* This belief may have been forged in a fast-moving environment — a startup, a high-pressure sales culture, a kitchen line where hesitation really did cost you — where speed was genuinely rewarded. The problem is that the situations requiring your leadership now are almost never solved by speed alone. They require regulation first, then decision.

The Disconnector often carries a belief that sounds like: *If I stay quiet and stay calm, I'm protecting my team. My composure is a gift to them.* What they miss is that their silence doesn't read as composure from the outside. It reads as distance. And teams operating under uncertainty, without a clear signal from their leader, will fill that silence with fear.

None of these beliefs are wrong, exactly. They're outdated. They were adaptive once. They've been running on autopilot long past the point where they serve you. And the first step to changing them is naming them — clearly, specifically, without the softening that makes them easy to ignore.

How to Map Your Own Pressure Profile

I want to give you a practical process for discovering your pressure profile with the kind of specificity that actually leads to change. This isn't a personality quiz. It's a structured self-inquiry — the same process I use with executive coaching clients in our first engagement.

Step One: Identify Your Last Three Pressure Moments

Go back in time — not to your entire career, but to the last six to twelve months. Identify three specific moments where pressure hit and you defaulted. Not moments where you performed perfectly under pressure. Moments where pressure revealed something you'd rather not see.

Write each one down in two to three sentences. Just the facts. What happened, and what you did.

Step Two: Name the Pattern

For each of those three moments, identify which of the four defaults showed up. Did you tighten control? Avoid the issue? React from emotion? Go quiet and disconnect?

You may see the same pattern repeat across all three. That's your dominant default. You may see two patterns — often a primary and a secondary that shows up when the primary doesn't resolve the pressure. That's important data too.

Step Three: Identify Your Primary Pressure Arena

Look at those three moments and ask: where did they happen? Were they all decision pressure situations — moments requiring clarity with incomplete data? Were they conflict pressure moments — human tension, difficult conversations, team dynamics? Were they performance pressure moments — results, revenue, accountability?

Your primary pressure arena is where your nervous system is most reliably triggered. And it's where the Pressure Performance System will give you the most immediate return.

Step Four: Find the Belief Underneath

This is the step most leaders skip — and it's the one that matters most. For each of your three pressure moments, ask: What did I believe in that moment that made my default feel like the right response?

Not what you knew rationally. What you believed in your body, in your gut, in the split second before you thought.

Write it down in one sentence. Keep it simple. *I believed that if I didn't fix this myself, it would fall apart. I believed that speaking up would make things worse. I believed that slowing down meant losing.*

That sentence — that belief — is your identity trigger. And it is the most important piece of data in your pressure profile.

Speed feels like decisiveness, but reaction without regulation is just chaos with authority.

What to Do With What You Find

Here's what I want you to know before we go any further: whatever you find in this process, it does not define you. Your pressure default is not a character verdict. It's a starting point. And the leaders who transform their performance under pressure are not the ones who had the cleanest starting point — they're the ones who looked at their starting point with the most honesty.

I've worked with executives who had been running a Controller default for thirty years and completely rewired their leadership identity in eighteen months of consistent work. I've worked with Avoiders who spent a decade postponing difficult conversations and then became the most courageous communicators on their executive teams. I've worked with Reactors who turned explosive tendencies into powerful, rapid-decision capability once they learned to regulate first.

The pattern is not the prison. The pattern is just the door you walk through when the pressure comes. And with the right system, you get to choose a different door.

That's what the next three chapters are about. The Pressure Performance System's three pillars — Identity Clarity, Emotional Regulation, and Execution Discipline — each address a specific layer of your pressure profile. Identity Clarity addresses the belief underneath the pattern. Emotional Regulation addresses the nervous system response that fires before the belief even has time to surface. Execution Discipline addresses the behavioral systems that let you perform consistently, regardless of what your nervous system is doing.

Together, they don't just change how you perform under pressure. They change who you are under pressure. And that difference — between performance change and identity change — is the difference between a leader who has a good quarter and a leader who elevates for the rest of their career.

A Note on Self-Compassion as a Leadership Discipline

Before we move into Part Two of this book, I want to say something that doesn't show up often enough in executive leadership literature: this work requires self-compassion. Not as a soft concept or a wellness talking point — but as a genuine leadership discipline.

The leaders who make the fastest progress through the Pressure Performance System are not the ones who are hardest on themselves about their defaults. They're the ones who can look at their patterns with the same clear, non-judgmental curiosity they'd bring to a business problem. *Here's what's happening. Here's why. Here's what needs to change. Let's build a system for it.*

Self-criticism under pressure is just another form of misalignment. It pulls you into the survival brain just as surely as external threat do. And a leader beating themselves up for being a Controller or an Avoider is a leader who has now added self-punishment to the list of things their nervous system needs to manage.

Look at what pressure reveals in you with honesty. Look at it with respect for the version of you that developed those patterns for good reasons. And then bring the same commitment to building something better that you bring to every other performance challenge in your business.

You wouldn't tell your best leader that their development area makes them fundamentally broken. Don't tell yourself that either.

Pressure Reflection: Chapter 4

Take time with these before moving forward. The Pressure Performance System is built on self-knowledge, and the quality of that self-knowledge determines the quality of everything that follows.

Question One:

Which of the four pressure defaults — Controller, Avoider, Reactor, Disconnector — most accurately describes your dominant pattern? If you're not sure, ask someone who has seen you under significant pressure. They already know. Give them permission to tell you.

Question Two:

Which of the five pressure arenas — Decision, Conflict, Negotiation, Change, Performance — fires your default most reliably? Where do you feel the pressure in your body before you even have time to think?

Question Three:

What is the belief underneath your default? Write it in one sentence, in first person, present tense. *I believe that… I believe that… I believe that…* Don't overwrite it. The simpler, the more honest.

Question Four:

When did that belief serve you? Where did it come from, and what did it help you survive or succeed at? Give it the respect it deserves.

Question Five:

What is that belief costing you now? In your leadership. In your relationships. In your performance under the specific kinds of pressure you face today.

Question Six:

If you could replace that belief with one that actually serves who you are becoming as a leader — what would it say? Write that sentence too. That's not just an affirmation. That's the beginning of your new identity under pressure.

In Part Two, we build the system that makes that new identity real — not just on paper, but in the moments that matter most.

"The pattern is not the prison. The pattern is just the door you walk through when the pressure comes."

— *Elevate Under Pressure*, Chapter 4

PART TWO
THE PRESSURE PERFORMANCE SYSTEM

5
THE SYSTEM

Pressure doesn't break leaders. It exposes what's already there.

By now, you know that. You've seen it in the stories. You've seen it in yourself. You've named your pressure default. You've identified the beliefs driving it. You've looked at what pressure has been revealing about your identity for years — and you've started to see it clearly, maybe for the first time.

And if you're like most of the leaders I work with, there's a question forming right now:

Okay. I see it. Now what do I do about it?

That's the right question. And it's where everything changes.

Part One of this book was about awareness. It was about understanding what pressure actually does to leaders, where misalignment happens, and how your specific pressure profile shapes your defaults under heat. That awareness is foundational. Without it, nothing else works.

But awareness alone doesn't change how you perform.

Part Two is about activation. This is where we move from understanding pressure to operating inside it. This is where you go from knowing your pattern to having a system that rewires it — in real time, under real conditions, when it actually matters.

The System

When pressure rises, leaders don't rise to the occasion. They default to their conditioning.

That's the fundamental truth I've observed across forty years of high-pressure environments — from kitchen lines to boardrooms, from ultramarathons to partnership dissolutions, from coaching sessions to caregiving. The leaders who perform brilliantly under pressure aren't performing from willpower or talent or some innate toughness. They're performing from trained conditioning. They've built something inside themselves that holds fast when everything around them is breaking down.

This isn't a philosophy. It's not a theory about what great leaders should do. It's a system — built from real experience, refined through hundreds of coaching engagements, and designed to work in the exact moments where most leadership development falls apart: when the pressure is real, the stakes are high, and there's no time to think about what you learned in a seminar.

The Pressure Performance System™ is simple.

Four moves.
One sequence.
Executed under pressure.

The Four Moves inside the moment itself.

Regulate — Name it. Slow it. Choose your state before you choose your response.

Reframe — Shift from threat to challenge. Take control of the narrative.

Decide — Anchor in identity and values. Move with clarity, not reaction.

Execute — Follow through with discipline. Protect standards. Deliver under pressure.

Simple. Not easy. Trainable.

Each of these moves addresses a specific failure point I've watched leaders hit under pressure, again and again. The leader who can't regulate fires from their survival brain. The leader who can't reframe stays trapped in the threat. The leader who can't decide hesitates until the moment decides for them. The leader who can't execute folds when the follow-through gets hard.

The sequence matters. You cannot reframe clearly from a survival state. You cannot decide wisely from panic. You cannot execute with discipline from adrenaline. Regulation comes first because it makes everything else possible.

This is the operating system. Four moves. One sequence. Designed to activate under the exact conditions that shut most leaders down.

When pressure rises, leaders don't rise to the occasion. They default to their conditioning.

Why Most Leaders Fail Under Pressure

Here's something I want you to sit with, because it redefines the entire conversation about leadership development:

Most leaders don't fail because they don't know what to do. They fail because, under pressure, they can't access what they know.

Think about that. The executive who knows the right decision but can't pull the trigger because her nervous system is flooded with threat signals. The founder who's read every book on difficult conversations but still avoids the one that matters because the emotional cost feels too high at the moment. The COO who has a clear strategic vision but micromanages when revenue dips because survival brain overrides strategic brain.

These leaders aren't unskilled. They aren't untrained. They've been to the workshops. They've done the leadership assessments. They know the frameworks.

But knowledge that doesn't hold under pressure isn't knowledge. It's a theory. And theory breaks the moment the heat gets real.

This is the gap that most leadership development never addresses. It teaches leaders what to do in ideal conditions and then sends them into conditions that are anything but ideal. It builds competency in the classroom and watches it evaporate in the boardroom. It gives leaders the playbook and then wonders why they can't run the plays when someone is rushing them from the blind side.

The Pressure Performance System was built specifically to close that gap. Not by giving you more knowledge. By giving you a system you can access *when your knowledge goes offline.*

What Makes the System Work

The four moves are the visible system — what you do under pressure. But they only work if something deeper is in place.

Every leader who performs consistently under pressure has built three internal conditions. These aren't skills you learn once. They're capacities you develop and strengthen over time — the foundation that makes the four moves possible.

> **Identity Clarity** — knowing who you are, what you stand for, and what drives your decisions *before* the pressure hits. When identity is clear, decisions stabilize. You stop making choices from fear, politics, or the need to be liked — and start making them from a grounded sense of who you are as a leader.

Emotional Regulation — the trained ability to recognize when your nervous system is taking over and to bring your thinking brain back online. When emotional regulation is strong, your state stabilizes. You stop reacting from cortisol and adrenaline — and start responding from clarity and composure.

Execution Discipline — the systems, habits, and practices that let you follow through consistently, not just when you feel motivated or when the pressure temporarily lifts. When execution discipline is built, your follow-through stabilizes. You stop performing in bursts — and start delivering with the kind of reliability that earns real trust.

Think of the three conditions as the infrastructure underneath the system. The four moves are what you do at the moment. The three conditions are who you've become that allows you to do it.

Without identity clarity, you'll regulate your state but still make the wrong decision because you don't know what you actually stand for. Without emotional regulation, you'll have the clarity but your nervous system will override it the moment threat appears. Without execution discipline, you'll think clearly and regulate beautifully and then fail to follow through when the work gets hard.

You need all three. And they need the four moves to activate them. One without the other gives you insight without performance, or performance without sustainability.

Together, they give you both.

The Integrated System

Let me give you the complete picture, because this is the architecture that everything in the rest of this book is built on:

It builds the internal conditions of identity clarity, emotional regulation, and execution discipline — and activates them in real time through four moves: regulate, reframe, decide, and execute.

Four moves that drive performance under pressure. Built on three conditions that make it sustainable.

That's the system. The rest of this book is about making it yours.

What This Looks Like in Practice

Let me make this concrete. Because systems only matter if they work where it counts.

Picture this: You're a VP of Operations. You've just walked into a quarterly review. The numbers are down — not catastrophically, but enough that the room is tense. Your CEO is visibly frustrated. Your peers are positioning themselves to deflect blame. Your direct reports are watching to see how you respond. And the data you're about to present doesn't have the answer everyone wants.

Here's what most leaders do in that room:

The Controller takes over. Starts rapid-firing solutions before anyone has even finished diagnosing the problem. Signals to the team that their input doesn't matter. Walks out having "fixed" the meeting but having lost the room.

The Avoider softens the numbers. Presents the data in the most favorable light. Defers the hard questions. Walks out relieved but having lost credibility with anyone paying attention.

The Reactor gets sharp. Challenges the CEO's frustration. Pushes back defensively on the numbers. Turns a tense meeting into a confrontation. Walks out having "stood their ground" but having damaged relationships that will take months to repair.

The Disconnector goes quiet. Presents the data flatly. Doesn't engage with the tension. Doesn't lead the room through the discomfort. Walks out unscathed but having done nothing to move the team forward.

Now here's what the system does differently.

Regulate. Before you walk in, or the moment you feel your nervous system fire, you name what's happening. I'm feeling threatened. My survival brain is activating. I'm about to default. You slow your breathing. You choose your state. You walk into that room from your thinking brain, not your survival brain.

Reframe. You shift the narrative. This isn't a room where you're being judged. This is a room where the team needs leadership. The numbers aren't an indictment — they're data. And data is the starting point for decision, not the end point of blame.

Decide. You anchor in your identity and values. You know who you are as a leader. You know what you stand for. And from that grounded place, you make a clear call: here's what the data says, here's what I recommend, here's what I need from each of you. No hedging. No politicking. Clarity.

Execute. You follow through. After the meeting, you don't retreat. You don't ruminate. You implement what you committed to. You hold the conversations that need to happen. You protect the standard, even when the pressure to soften it is real.

Same room. Same pressure. Completely different outcome. Not because you had more information or better talent or a thicker skin. Because you had a system.

Knowledge that doesn't hold under pressure isn't knowledge. It's theory. And theory breaks the moment the heat gets real.

What's Ahead

In the chapters ahead, we're going to break down each move of the Pressure Performance System — so you don't just understand how it works, you can *apply* it when it matters most. You'll learn how to regulate your nervous system in real time. How to reframe high-pressure situations from threat to challenge. How to make clear, identity-driven decisions under conditions that break most leaders. And how to execute with the kind of discipline that earns trust and delivers results — especially when things get hard.

This isn't going to be theoretical. Every chapter will give you specific, practical tools you can use immediately — in your next meeting, your next difficult conversation, your next high-stakes moment.

Because that's what this system was built for. Not the seminar. Not the retreat. The moment.

The moment when pressure hits, the room is watching, and you have a choice: default to your conditioning, or activate the system.

Let's build the system.

Pressure Reflection: Chapter 5

Before moving into the deep work of each move, take a few minutes with these questions. They're designed to connect what you've just read to the pressure reality you're living right now.

Question One:

Think about the four moves — Regulate, Reframe, Decide, Execute. Which one do you sense is your weakest link under pressure? Not in general — under *real* pressure. Which move breaks down first when the heat comes? That's where your system is most vulnerable, and it's where the work ahead will give you the most immediate return.

Question Two:

Consider the three conditions — Identity Clarity, Emotional Regulation, Execution Discipline. Which one feels most underdeveloped in your leadership right now? Where's the gap in your foundation? The condition that's weakest is usually the one that explains why the move above keeps failing.

Question Three:

Go back to the quarterly review scenario — or replace it with a high-pressure moment from your own recent experience. Walk through the four moves in your mind. What would Regulate look like for you at that moment? Reframe? Decide? Execute? Be specific. The more precisely you can imagine the moves, the more accessible they'll become when the pressure is real.

Question Four:

What is the pressure moment you know is coming in the next thirty days? A conversation, a decision, a performance challenge, a transition. Name it. That's your live training ground for everything in Part Two. You're not learning this system in the abstract. You're learning it for *that* moment.

In the next chapter, we go deep on the first move — Regulate — because everything else in the system depends on it. Without regulation, there is no reframe. Without reframe, there is no decision. Without decision, there is no execution. It starts here.

— *Elevate Under Pressure*, Chapter 5

6
REGULATE — CHOOSE YOUR STATE BEFORE YOU CHOOSE YOUR RESPONSE

There's a moment in the kitchen I've never forgotten.

I was seventeen. Friday night. One hundred covers (reservations) on the books. The sous chef had just walked off the line — personal crisis, no warning, gone. The head chef looked at me and said two words: You're up.

I was not ready. I knew I was not ready. And my body knew it before my brain did. Heart rate spiked. Hands went cold. My vision narrowed to the six tickets already hanging on the rail. Every sound in that kitchen got louder and closer at the same time.

I had a choice at that moment. I didn't know to call it regulation then, but that's exactly what it was. I could let my survival brain take the wheel — rush the first plate, bark at the line, try to look like I had it together while my nervous system was screaming. Or I could do what I'd watched the best cooks do when the tickets stacked up and the room caught fire.

I took one breath. I read the first ticket. I said the first order out loud, calmly, to the line. And I moved.

Not fast. Not slow. Regulated.

That's the move. That's the first and most foundational move in the Pressure Performance System. And forty years later, it's still the one that makes everything else possible.

Why Regulation Is the Master Skill

In Chapter 5, I introduced the four moves of the Pressure Performance System: Regulate, Reframe, Decide, Execute. I told you the sequence matters. Now I want to show you why.

When pressure hits, your brain doesn't wait for your permission to respond. Your amygdala — the threat-detection center that's been keeping humans alive for hundreds of thousands of years — fires in milliseconds. Cortisol and adrenaline flood your system. Your prefrontal cortex — the part of your brain responsible for strategic thinking, emotional nuance, and clear decision-making — begins to go offline.

This happens to every human being. Every leader. Every time.

The question is not whether your survival brain will activate under pressure. It will. The question is whether you have the tools to recognize that activation and bring your thinking brain back online before you say the thing, send the email, make the decision. If not, you may spend the next three months or more trying to rebuild the relationships.

That's regulation. And without it, the rest of the system is inaccessible.

You cannot reframe a situation when your brain is interpreting everything as a threat. You cannot make a clear, identity-anchored decision when your nervous system is flooded with cortisol. You cannot execute with discipline when adrenaline is driving your behavior. Every move in this system depends on your ability to regulate first.

This is why I call regulation the master skill. Not because it's the most complex. Because it's the gateway. Get this right, and everything else becomes possible. Skip it, and nothing else holds.

What Regulation Is Not

Before we go further, I want to clear something up. Because the word "regulation" carries baggage in leadership circles, and most of it is wrong.

Regulation is not suppression. It is not stuffing your emotions down, putting on a calm face, and pretending you're fine when you're not. That's performance. And performance without regulation is just a more polished version of your survival default.

Regulation is not relaxation. I'm not asking you to meditate in the middle of a board meeting or take a bubble bath before your next difficult conversation. Regulation is a real-time, in-the-moment discipline. It works in the hallway before the meeting. In the three seconds between reading the email and hitting reply. In the pause between the provocation and the response.

Regulation is not weakness. This is the one comment I hear most from the leaders I coach, especially the ones who've built their careers on speed and decisiveness. *If I slow down, I lose my edge. If I regulate, I'm soft.* The opposite is true. The fastest, sharpest, most decisive leaders I've ever worked with are the ones who regulate first. They're not slower. They're more accurate. They're not softer. They're more precise. They're leading from their thinking brain instead of their survival brain, and the difference in their decisions, their communication, and their impact is unmistakable.

Regulation is a leadership discipline. Full stop. The most composed leaders you've ever seen weren't born that way. They built it. And composure under pressure — real composure, not performed composure — is the single most powerful signal a leader can send to their team.

Your tone becomes culture. Your state becomes the room's state. When you're regulated, the people around you can think. When you're not, they can't. It's that direct.

Your regulation is contagious.
So is your dysregulation.

The Three Signals: How to Know Your Survival Brain Has Taken Over

Regulation starts with recognition. You can't regulate what you can't see. And one of the most common reasons leaders fail to regulate under pressure is that they don't recognize the activation until it's already driving their behavior.

Your body will always tell you before your mind does. The survival brain fires faster than the thinking brain can process. So the first skill of regulation is learning to read the signals your body is sending before your mouth opens or your fingers hit the keyboard.

There are three signals to watch for. Every leader's version is slightly different, but the pattern is universal.

Signal One: The Physical Shift

This is the most immediate and the easiest to catch once you know what you're looking for. Heart rate increases. Breathing becomes shallow and moves to the upper chest. Jaw tightens. Shoulders rise. Hands go cold or restless. Stomach knots. Some leaders describe it as a band tightening across the chest. Others feel heat in their face or neck.

Your version may be different, but you have one. And once you learn to recognize it, it becomes the earliest, most reliable signal that your survival brain is coming online.

Signal Two: The Cognitive Narrowing

When the survival brain activates, your field of perception narrows. You stop seeing the full picture and start fixating on the threat. In a meeting, this might show up as losing track of the broader agenda and locking onto the one comment that felt like a challenge. In a negotiation, it's fixating on the other side's aggression instead of the strategic position. In a crisis, it's jumping to the first available solution instead of assessing the actual problem.

Cognitive narrowing feels like focus. It isn't. It's tunnel vision driven by threat, and the decisions that come from it are almost always reactive, premature, or incomplete.

Signal Three: The Emotional Acceleration

This is the one that shows up in your communication. Your tone sharpens. Your patience contracts. Your language gets more absolute — always, never, everyone, no one. You start interpreting neutral events as hostile. A colleague's question becomes a challenge. A team member's silence becomes resistance. A client's email becomes a threat.

When your emotional interpretation is accelerating faster than the situation warrants, your survival brain is driving. And anything you say, write, or decide from that state will carry the imprint of threat — whether the threat is real or not.

These three signals — physical shift, cognitive narrowing, emotional acceleration — are your early warning system. The leaders who regulate well aren't the ones who never get triggered. They're the ones who catch the trigger within seconds instead of minutes. And seconds is all you need.

The Regulation Protocol: Name It. Slow It. Choose It.

This is a practical tool. This is what you're going to use in the hallway, in the meeting, in the three-second window between the trigger and your response. I call it the Regulation Protocol, and it has three steps.

Step One: Name It

The moment you recognize one of the three signals, name what's happening. Internally. Silently. In plain language.

My survival brain just activated. I'm in threat mode. My body is ahead of my brain right now.

That's it. One sentence. The naming itself is a regulatory act — neuroscience calls this *affect labeling,* and it's one of the most well-documented tools for interrupting the amygdala's hijack of the prefrontal cortex. When you name what's happening, you create a micro-gap between the stimulus and the response. You move from being *inside* the reaction to *observing* it. And from that observer position, you have choice.

Most leaders skip this step. They go straight to managing the situation — which means they're managing it from a dysregulated state. Naming comes first because it's what gives you access to everything else.

Step Two: Slow It

Once you've named the activation, you slow the nervous system's momentum. This is the physiological intervention — and it works faster than most leaders believe possible.

The primary tool is breath. Specifically, a deliberate extension of the exhale. When your exhale is longer than your inhale, your vagus nerve activates the parasympathetic response — the branch of your nervous system responsible for calming, recovering, and returning to baseline. This is not a theory. This is the physiological mechanism your body uses to shift from survival mode to recovery mode.

Here's the protocol I teach my clients and use myself:

> **The 4-6 Reset** — Inhale through the nose for a count of four. Exhale through the mouth for a count of six. Two to three cycles. It takes less than thirty seconds. Can be done in any room, any meeting, any conversation without anyone noticing.

That's it. Two to three breaths. Less than thirty seconds. And in those thirty seconds, your prefrontal cortex begins to come back online. Your heart rate starts to lower. Your cognitive field starts to widen. You are, in the most literal neurological sense, giving your thinking brain access to the situation again.

For leaders who need a faster intervention — the moment where you have maybe five seconds before you need to speak — there's an even simpler version:

> **The Exhale Reset** — One long, slow exhale. Twice as long as feels natural. Drop the shoulders on the exhale. That single breath activates the parasympathetic response and buys you the cognitive space to choose your next move.

I've used the Exhale Reset on kitchen lines, in boardrooms, in conversations with my wife's care team, and on mountain ridges at altitude where panic was not an option. It works. Every time. Not because it's magic. Because it's biology.

Step Three: Choose It

This is where regulation becomes leadership.

Once you've named the activation and slowed the nervous system, you have something most leaders never access under pressure: choice. You can now choose your state before you choose your response.

Ask yourself one question:

Who do I need to be at this moment?

Not what I need to do. Who do I need to be. Because the doing will follow the being. If you choose to be the leader who holds the room steady, your words will reflect that. If you choose to be the leader who asks the clear question instead of reacting to the sharp comment, your tone will reflect that. If you choose to be the leader who slows the conversation down when everyone else is accelerating, your presence will do the work.

Name it. Slow it. Choose it. That's the Regulation Protocol. Three steps. Thirty seconds or less. And it is the most important thirty seconds in your leadership.

Building Your Somatic Awareness: The Baseline Practice

The Regulation Protocol works at the moment. But the leaders who regulate most effectively under pressure are the ones who've done something else first: they've built a baseline awareness of their body's signals before the pressure hits.

I call this somatic awareness — the practice of knowing what your body is doing before your mind has time to interpret it. And it's the difference between catching the activation in three seconds versus three minutes.

This is work I've done extensively with leaders, and it's informed by years of partnership with somatic practitioners who bring trauma-sensitive, body-based approaches to leadership development. It's not esoteric. It's practical. And it builds faster than most leaders expect.

Here's the baseline practice:

The Body Scan Check-In

Twice a day — once in the morning, once before your most significant meeting or conversation — take sixty seconds and run a simple scan. Start at the top of your head and move down. What's tight? What's holding? Where's the tension sitting today?

You're not trying to fix anything. You're not trying to relax. You're building the habit of noticing. Because the leader who knows what their body feels like at baseline is the leader who immediately recognizes when that baseline shifts under pressure.

Over time, this sixty-second practice builds what I think of as an internal dashboard. You start to know your signals the way a pilot knows their instrument panel. Jaw tight — that's frustration. Chest tight — that's anxiety. Shoulders rising — that's protection mode. Shallow breathing — that's survival brain coming online.

You don't have to analyze it. You just have to see it. The seeing is the regulation.

Regulation in Practice: Three Scenarios

Let me show you how this works in the moments that actually matter.

The Reactive Email

You open an email from a board member. The tone is sharp. They're questioning a decision you made last quarter. Your chest tightens. Your jaw sets. Your fingers are already moving toward the keyboard.

The old pattern: you draft a response immediately. It's thorough, detailed, and underneath the professionalism, it's defensive. You send it. Two hours later, you wish you'd waited.

The regulated response: You catch the physical shift — chest, jaw, hands. You name it: *survival brain, threat mode.* You close the laptop. You take two 4-6 Reset breaths. You ask yourself: *Who do I need to be in this response?* You decide: the leader who responds from strategic clarity, not emotional defense. You draft the email an hour later. It's shorter, clearer, and carries the authority of composure instead of the heat of reaction.

Same email. Same board member. Completely different outcome. The only variable was thirty seconds of regulation.

Your tone becomes culture. Your state becomes the room's state.

The Meeting That Turns

You're leading a strategy session. One of your VPs pushes back hard on your proposal. Their tone is sharp. The room shifts. You feel the emotional acceleration — your interpretation of their pushback jumps from *disagreement* to *disrespect* in less than a second.

The old pattern: you match their energy. You go sharp. You defend the proposal with force instead of clarity. The VP digs in. The meeting becomes a power struggle. The rest of the team goes silent.

The regulated response: You catch the emotional acceleration. You name it. You take one Exhale Reset before you speak. You choose your state: *I'm the leader who holds the room, not the one who wins the argument.* You respond with a question instead of a defense: "Help me understand what you're seeing that I'm not." The VP's energy shifts because yours did first. The room opens back up. The conversation gets productive.

Your regulation became the room's regulation. That's not a metaphor. That's mirror neurons. Your state is contagious, and under pressure, the leader's state sets the ceiling for the entire team's capacity to think.

The Caregiving Morning

I want to give you a personal one, because regulation isn't just a boardroom skill. It's a life skill.

There are mornings in my caregiving reality where the pressure arrives before I've finished my first cup of coffee. A difficult moment with my wife. A call from my mother's care team. A weight that settles in and doesn't announce when it plans to leave. And on those mornings, I have coaching sessions. I have client commitments. I have leadership work that requires me to show up fully present for someone else's pressure.

The Regulation Protocol is how I make that transition. I name what's happening: *I'm carrying weight today. My nervous system is activated. I'm not in a coaching state yet.* I slow it: the 4-6 Reset, sometimes five or six cycles instead of two. I choose it: *Who do I need to be for this client in the next hour?* And I step into the session from that choice — not from the weight.

Regulation doesn't make the weight disappear. It gives me the capacity to lead alongside it. And that's what I want for you. Not a life without pressure. A life where pressure doesn't get to decide who you are.

The Daily Regulation Practice

Regulation under pressure is built in the moments outside of pressure. Like any skill, it compounds with practice. And the good news is that the practice doesn't require an hour a day or a meditation retreat. It requires consistency and intention.

Here's the daily practice I recommend for every leader I work with:

Morning: The 60-Second Body Scan

Before you check your phone, before you open your inbox, take sixty seconds to scan your body from head to feet. Notice what's present. Notice what's tight.

Set your baseline for the day. This is your instrument check before takeoff.

Pre-Engagement: The 4-6 Reset

Before your most significant meeting, conversation, or decision of the day, take thirty seconds and run two to three cycles of the 4-6 breath. You're not trying to calm down. You're deliberately activating your parasympathetic nervous system so your thinking brain is fully online when you need it most.

In-the-Moment: The Exhale Reset

When you feel any of the three signals — physical shift, cognitive narrowing, emotional acceleration — take one long exhale. Drop the shoulders. Buy yourself three seconds of cognitive space. Then choose.

End of Day: The State Review

Take two minutes at the end of your day to reflect: Where did I regulate well today? Where did my survival brain drive a decision, a conversation, or a tone before I caught it? No judgment. Just data. Over time, this review shortens the gap between trigger and regulation from minutes to seconds.

Four touchpoints. Less than five minutes total. And they fundamentally change how your nervous system responds to pressure — not by eliminating the response, but by giving you the awareness and the tools to choose what comes next.

From Technique to Identity

Here's what I want you to understand about regulation, because this is where it connects back to everything we built in Part One.

Regulation is not just a technique you use in high-pressure moments. Over time, it becomes part of who you are as a leader. The executive who has built a daily regulation practice doesn't walk into a crisis and think, *I need to regulate now.* They walk in already regulated. Their baseline has shifted. Their nervous system's default response has changed — not because the pressure changed, but because they changed.

This is the deeper point of the Pressure Performance System. The four moves aren't just things you do. They're things you become. And regulation — the ability to choose your state before you choose your response — is the foundation of that becoming.

Remember what I said in Chapter 4: the three internal conditions are the invisible infrastructure that makes the visible system work. Emotional Regulation is the condition underneath this move. And the daily practice I just gave you is how you build it — not overnight, not in a workshop, but through the accumulated discipline of choosing your state a thousand times until choosing becomes who you are.

That's the real goal. Not a leader who regulates when they remember to. A leader whose regulated state is their default — because they've trained it that deeply.

What's Ahead

Regulation gives you access. It brings your thinking brain back online and gives you the cognitive space to lead instead of react. But what you do with that space matters enormously.

In the next chapter, we're going to work on the second move: Reframe. Because once you're regulated — once your survival brain is no longer driving — you need to change how you're interpreting the pressure itself. The difference between a leader who sees a crisis as a threat and a leader who sees it as a challenge is not personality. It's a trained reframe. And it changes everything about what happens next.

Regulation *with*out reframe gives you composure. Regulation with reframe gives you leverage.

Let's build both.

Pressure Reflection: Chapter 6

These questions are designed to move regulation from a concept into your actual leadership practice. Take time with them.

Question One:

What are your personal versions of the three signals? When your survival brain activates, where do you feel it first in your body? How does your thinking narrow? How does your emotional interpretation shift? Be specific. The more precisely you can describe your signals, the faster you'll catch them.

Question Two:

Think about the last time you responded to pressure before you were regulated. What happened? What did that cost you — in the relationship, the decision, the room's energy? Now replay that moment with the Regulation Protocol. What would have been different if you'd taken thirty seconds?

Question Three:

Practice the 4-6 Reset right now. Inhale for four, exhale for six. Three cycles. Notice what shifts in your body. That shift — however subtle — is your parasympathetic response activating. That's the mechanism that will bring your thinking brain back online under pressure.

Question Four:

Commit to the Daily Regulation Practice for the next seven days. Morning body scan. Pre-engagement 4-6 Reset. In-the-moment Exhale Reset when you catch a signal. End-of-day State Review. Track what you notice. The data from those seven days will show you exactly where your regulation is strong and where the work needs to go.

Question Five:

What is the high-pressure moment coming in your next two weeks where regulation will matter most? Name it. Visualize yourself running the Regulation Protocol inside that moment. See yourself naming the activation, slowing the breath, choosing your state. The more vividly you rehearse it now, the more accessible it will be when the pressure is real.

In the next chapter, we move to the second move — Reframe — because regulation opens the door, but how you see the situation on the other side of that door determines everything.

"Your regulation is contagious. So is your dysregulation."

— *Elevate Under Pressure*, Chapter 6

7
REFRAME — SHIFT FROM THREAT TO CHALLENGE

In 2024, I experienced one of the most significant personal betrayals of my life.

I'm not going to give you the details here — that's not the point. The point is what happened inside me when it hit. Because the betrayal wasn't just emotional. It was structural. It threatened relationships, revenue, and my sense of who I could trust. It arrived in the middle of an already full life — clients depending on me, caregiving responsibilities that didn't pause, and a body of work I was actively building.

I regulated. I used the tools you read about in the last chapter. I named the activation. I slowed my nervous system. I chose my state before I chose my response.

But regulation alone wasn't enough. Because even with a regulated nervous system, I was still seeing the situation through a lens of threat. Every conversation felt loaded. Every email looked suspicious. Every new interaction was filtered through the question: *Is this going to hurt me too?*

My thinking brain was back online. But it was thinking from the wrong frame.

That's when I learned something about the second move of the Pressure Performance System that I'd understood intellectually but had never felt so viscerally: regulation gives you access to your thinking brain. Reframing gives you access to your *best* thinking brain. And those are not the same thing.

What Reframing Actually Is

Reframing is not positive thinking. I want to be direct about that, because the moment a leadership book mentions "reframing," most experienced executives check out. They've heard the motivational version. *See the silver lining. Every obstacle is an opportunity. Choose to see the glass as half full.* That's not what I'm talking about.

Reframing, as a move inside the Pressure Performance System, is a specific cognitive discipline: it's the trained ability to shift your interpretation of a high-pressure situation from a threat frame to a challenge frame.

Here's why that distinction matters — and it matters at the level of neuroscience, not just mindset.

When your brain interprets a situation as a threat, it mobilizes resources for defense. Blood flow shifts toward your large muscle groups. Your cognitive field narrows. Your creativity contracts. Your brain starts scanning for what could go wrong, what you might lose, who might be dangerous. You are, neurologically, in protection mode. You can think — regulation gave you that — but you're thinking defensively.

When your brain interprets the same situation as a **challenge**, it mobilizes resources for performance. Blood flow increases to the brain. Your cognitive field opens. You start scanning for options, resources, and opportunities. You feel the pressure — the stakes are still real — but your system is oriented toward engagement rather than survival. You're thinking expansively.

Same situation. Same stakes. Same pressure. But two fundamentally different neurological states — and two fundamentally different qualities of leadership that follow from them.

The leader who sees a quarterly shortfall as a threat micromanages, tightens control, and signals panic. The leader who sees the same shortfall as a challenge asks better questions, engages the team's thinking, and finds solutions that a threat-oriented brain would never access.

The leader who sees a team conflict as a threat avoids it, defers it, or escalates it. The leader who sees the same conflict as a challenge names the real issue and leads through it — because challenge-oriented brains can hold discomfort without collapsing into survival.

Reframing is not pretending the pressure isn't real. It's changing your brain's relationship to the pressure so you can lead inside it instead of defending against it.

The Threat-Challenge Gap

Every high-pressure situation has both elements. There is something at stake — that's the threat. And there is something to be gained, solved, or led through — that's the challenge. Both are real. Neither is imagined.

The question is which one your brain leads with. And under pressure, without a trained reframe, your brain will almost always lead with the threat. That's not pessimism. It's evolution. The survival brain is wired to prioritize danger over opportunity because, for most of human history, missing a threat was fatal and missing an opportunity was just inconvenient.

But in leadership, that wiring works against you. Because the decisions that define your career, your culture, and your organization are almost never made well from a threat frame. They require the cognitive breadth, creative capacity, and relational openness that only a challenge frame provides.

I call the distance between where your brain goes automatically and where it needs to go the Threat-Challenge Gap. And just like the Alignment Gap from Chapter 2, every leader has one. The leaders who consistently perform under pressure aren't the ones who naturally see challenges instead of threats. They're the ones who've trained the shift.

The story you tell yourself is the strategy you run. Master the story, and you master the response.

The Reframe Protocol: Three Questions That Change Everything

Here's the practical tool. Once you've regulated — once your thinking brain is back online and your survival brain is no longer driving — you run the Reframe Protocol. Three questions, asked internally, in sequence.

Question One: What's actually at stake here?

Not what your survival brain says is at stake. Not the catastrophic interpretation. The actual, concrete stakes.

When the board member sends a sharp email, your survival brain says: *My credibility is being destroyed. My position is at risk. They're coming for me.* The actual stakes? A board member has a question about a decision. That's it. That's what's actually happening.

When a key client signals they're considering a competitor, your survival brain says: *Revenue is collapsing. I'm failing. The business is in danger.* The actual stakes? One client relationship needs attention. The situation has a real cost, but it is not the extinction event your nervous system is making it feel like.

This question strips the narrative back to facts. Not feelings about facts. Facts. And from facts, you can lead. From fear-inflated narratives, you can only defend.

Question Two: Where's the leadership opportunity here?

This is the shift from threat to challenge. Once you've named the actual stakes, you ask: what does this situation require of me as a leader? Not what it threatens. What does it *require?*

The quarterly shortfall requires a leader who can engage the team in honest problem-solving instead of micromanaging from panic. That's a leadership opportunity.

The team conflict requires a leader who can name the real issue, hold the discomfort, and lead a group of smart people through tension to alignment. That's a leadership opportunity.

The negotiation where the other side is pushing hard requires a leader who can hold their position with composure and conviction while the room gets uncomfortable. That's a leadership opportunity.

Every high-pressure moment has one. And the moment you identify it, your brain shifts from *What am I defending against?* to *What am I leading toward?* That shift changes everything — your tone, your decisions, your presence, and the signal you send to everyone watching.

Question Three: Who do I want to be on the other side of this?

This is the question that connects the Reframe to Identity Clarity — the first of the three internal conditions.

Under threat, leaders make short-term decisions. They optimize for relief, not leadership. They do whatever makes the pressure stop, even if it costs them in the long run. This is why Controllers take over — it relieves the anxiety of uncertainty. This is why Avoiders defer — it relieves the anxiety of conflict. The threat frame drives leaders toward immediate emotional relief at the expense of long-term leadership integrity.

This question breaks that pattern. When you ask: "Who do I want to be on the other side of this?", you're no longer optimizing for relief. You're optimizing for identity. You're making the current moment serve the leader you're becoming, not the survival pattern you're leaving behind.

I used this question more times than I can count during the betrayal I mentioned at the opening of this chapter. When the old frame wanted to pull me into suspicion, self-protection, and withdrawal, I asked myself: *Who do I want to be when this chapter of my life is over?* And the answer was always the same: the leader who stayed open, who kept coaching at the highest level, who let the experience make him sharper instead of harder.

That answer didn't make the pressure disappear. But it changed how I moved through it. And the quality of every decision I made during that season was shaped by the frame, not the facts.

Three questions. *What's actually at stake? Where's the leadership opportunity? Who do I want to be on the other side of this?* That's the Reframe Protocol. Run it after regulation, and you will be thinking from your best brain — not just your thinking brain.

The Narrative Principle: The Story You Tell Is the Strategy You Run

There's a deeper layer to reframing that I want you to understand, because it explains why some leaders seem to handle enormous pressure with a kind of forward-moving energy while others get crushed by pressure that looks manageable from the outside.

The difference is narrative.

Every leader, in every pressure moment, is running a story. Most of the time, it's unconscious. It's the running internal commentary about what's happening, what it means, and what's going to happen next. And that narrative — not the situation itself — is what determines how the leader performs.

The leader whose internal narrative says *This is falling apart and I'm the one who has to hold it together alone* will perform from exhaustion, control, and isolation.

The leader whose internal narrative says *This is hard, and I have a team and a system and the capacity to lead through it* will perform from engagement, clarity, and collaboration.

Same situation. Different narrative. Completely different leadership.

The Reframe Protocol works because it intervenes at the narrative level. When you ask *What's actually at stake?* you're editing the narrative from catastrophe to reality. When you ask *Where's the leadership opportunity?* you're editing the narrative from defense to engagement. When you ask *Who do I want to be on the other side of this?* you're editing the narrative from survival to identity.

The story you tell yourself is the strategy you run. Master the story, and you master the response.

Reframing in Practice: Three Scenarios

Let me make this concrete. The same way I showed you regulation in practice in Chapter 6, I want to show you what the Reframe Protocol looks like in real leadership moments.

The Team Crisis That Isn't a Crisis

Your head of sales comes to you on a Thursday afternoon. Two enterprise deals that were supposed to close this quarter have stalled. The pipeline is suddenly thin. The tone of the message is urgent — bordering on panic.

Your survival brain fires. Threat frame activates: *We're going to miss the quarter. The board is going to push back. I need to fix this immediately.*

You regulate. Name it, slow it, choose your state.

Then you reframe.

What's actually at stake? Two deals have slowed — not died. The quarter is at risk, not the company. The board needs a clear narrative, not a miracle.

Where's the leadership opportunity? This is the moment to engage the sales leader in strategic problem-solving instead of taking over the deals myself. It's also a moment to build the team's capacity to manage pipeline pressure instead of depending on me to do it for them.

Who do I want to be on the other side of this? The leader who stayed steady, who equipped the team, and who built a stronger pipeline discipline because of this quarter, not in spite of it.

From that frame, your next conversation with the sales leader is completely different. Instead of micromanaging two deals, you're leading a strategic conversation about pipeline health. Instead of signaling panic, you're modeling composure. Instead of solving the problem alone, you're developing the people who need to solve it.

The Conflict That's Actually an Opportunity for Trust

Two of your senior leaders are in open disagreement about the direction of a major initiative. The tension is starting to leak into their teams. A meeting you facilitated last week ended with polite silence and zero alignment.

Threat frame: This is going to fracture the leadership team. *I need to pick a side or force a decision before it gets worse.*

You regulate. Then you reframe.

What's actually at stake? Two leaders disagree about a direction. Both have legitimate perspectives. The tension is uncomfortable, but it's not destructive — yet. What would make it destructive is avoidance, forced agreement, or a decision made from political pressure.

Where's the leadership opportunity? This is a trust-building moment. If I can lead these two leaders through a real disagreement — without avoiding it, without forcing it, without taking sides — the team's capacity for honest strategic debate gets permanently stronger.

Who do I want to be on the other side of this? The leader who held the space for real disagreement and helped the team come out aligned, not compliant.

From that frame, you don't avoid the next meeting. You design it. You name the disagreement openly. You create the conditions for honest debate. And you lead the room to alignment — which is fundamentally different from agreement. Alignment means we understand the decision, we understand the reasoning, and we're committed to executing even if it wasn't our preferred path. That only happens when a leader can reframe conflict from threat to opportunity.

The Board Meeting Where the Numbers Didn't Land

This is the public pressure moment from Chapter 2 — the one where the whole room is watching. The quarterly results are below target. The board is frustrated. The questions are pointed.

Threat frame: *I'm being judged. My competence is being questioned. I need to defend my decisions and make this look better than it is.*

You regulate. Then you reframe.

What's actually at stake? The numbers are what they are. The board deserves a clear explanation and a credible plan. My credibility isn't built on one quarter — it's built on how I lead *through* this quarter.

Where's the leadership opportunity? This is the moment where the board learns who I am under pressure. If I show up with clarity, ownership, and a plan, this quarter becomes a credibility-building moment. If I show up defensive, this quarter becomes the story they tell about me for the next year.

Who do I want to be on the other side of this? The leader the board trusts *more* after a tough quarter, not less.

From that frame, you don't defend. You own. You present the data clearly, name what contributed to the shortfall, and walk the board through a specific, time-bound plan to close the gap. Your tone is steady. Your composure signals competence. And the board walks out thinking, *That's a leader who can handle pressure* — which is exactly the signal that a threat frame would have destroyed.

Regulation without reframe gives you composure. Regulation with reframe gives you leverage.

The Compounding Effect of Reframing

Here's something I've observed across hundreds of coaching engagements that I want to share with you, because it's the part of reframing that most leaders don't see until they're months into the practice.

Reframing compounds.

The first time you use the Reframe Protocol, it takes effort. You have to consciously override the threat narrative and build a new one. It feels deliberate, maybe even forced.

The tenth time, it's faster. The questions come more naturally. You start catching the threat frame earlier — sometimes before it fully forms.

The hundredth time, something shifts fundamentally. Your default interpretation of pressure starts to change. You don't see the board meeting as a threat that you have to reframe into a challenge. You walk in already seeing it as a challenge. Your baseline narrative has shifted.

This is the move becoming identity. This is the technique becoming who you are. And this is where the second internal condition — Emotional Regulation

— intersects with Identity Clarity. Your identity as a leader expands to include this: *I am the kind of leader who sees pressure as a challenge, not a threat.* And once that becomes part of how you see yourself, the reframe is no longer a tool you use. It's how you see.

That's the goal. Not a leader who remembers to reframe. A leader whose default frame is challenge.

What's Ahead

You now have two moves working together. Regulation brings your thinking brain online. Reframing orients that brain toward challenge instead of threat. Together, they give you composure and clarity — the ability to be fully present in a high-pressure moment and see it accurately, not through the distortion of survival.

But composure and clarity aren't enough. You have to do something with them.

In the next chapter, we move to the third move: Decide. Because the moment of decision under pressure is where most leaders lose their nerve. Not because they can't think clearly. Not because they can't see the options. But because they haven't anchored their decision-making in something deeper than the pressure itself — their identity, their values, and a clarity about who they are that holds when everything else is moving.

Regulation gives you access. Reframing gives you clarity. Decision gives you direction.

Let's build the third move.

Pressure Reflection: Chapter 7

These questions are designed to train your reframe muscle. They work best if you use a real, current pressure situation — not a hypothetical.

Question One:

Think about the most significant pressure you're carrying right now. What's the story your brain is telling you about it? Write it down as honestly as you can, including the threat narrative. *This is going to… They're going to… I'm going to lose…* Don't edit it. Let the survival brain's narrative be visible on paper.

Question Two:

Now run the Reframe Protocol on that situation. *What's actually at stake?* Strip it to facts, not feelings about facts. Write the actual, concrete stakes in one or two sentences.

Question Three:

Where's the leadership opportunity? What does this situation require of you as a leader — not what does it threaten? What could this moment build in you, in your team, or in your organization if you led through it at your best?

Question Four:

Who do you want to be on the other side of this? Not what do you want to have accomplished. Who do you want to *be?* Write that identity in one sentence.

Question Five:

Compare the narrative from Question One with the frame you built in Questions Two through Four. Notice the distance. That distance is your Threat-Challenge Gap for this specific situation. The Reframe Protocol is how you close it — every time, in every moment, under any pressure.

Question Six:

Identify one conversation, meeting, or decision in the next seven days where you know your brain will default to a threat frame. Commit to running the Reframe Protocol before you walk into that room. After it's over, write down what was different. That data will teach you more about reframing than anything I can put on a page.

In the next chapter, we move to the third move — Decide — because once you can see the situation clearly, you need to be able to move. And the quality of your decisions under pressure is determined by something most leaders have never examined: the relationship between their identity and their choices.

"The story you tell yourself is the strategy you run. Master the story, and you master the response."

— *Elevate Under Pressure*, Chapter 7

8

DECIDE — ANCHOR IN IDENTITY AND VALUES. MOVE WITH CLARITY.

The hardest decision I ever made as a business owner was dissolving my partnership.

Not because the decision was unclear. By the time the moment came, I knew. The partnership was no longer working. The misalignment was structural, not circumstantial, and no amount of effort was going to fix what had broken at the foundation. The data was clear. The pattern was clear. The cost of continuing was clear.

The decision was hard because of everything *around* the decision. The financial exposure. The relational fallout. The employees who depended on both of us. The identity I'd built as someone who finishes what he starts, who doesn't walk away, who finds a way to make things work. Dissolving the partnership didn't just threaten my business. It threatened my story about who I was.

And that's the part most people miss about decision-making under pressure. The hard part is almost never the decision itself. It's the identity cost. It's the moment where making the right call requires you to let go of the story you've been telling yourself about who you are — and step into a version of yourself that the pressure is demanding you become.

I made the decision. I dissolved the partnership. It was painful, expensive, and it changed the trajectory of my career. And it was the right call — not because it was easy, but because it was aligned. Aligned with my values. Aligned with who I needed to be as a leader. Aligned with the truth I'd been avoiding because the cost of seeing it felt too high.

That's the third move. Decide. And it's the one that separates leaders who perform well under pressure from leaders who transform under it.

Why Leaders Struggle With Decisions Under Pressure

Here's what I've observed working with executives through hundreds of high-stakes decision moments: the leaders who struggle most with decisions under pressure are not the ones who lack information. They're the ones who lack clarity about who they are.

When identity is unclear, every decision becomes a negotiation. Not a negotiation with the data or the stakeholders — a negotiation with yourself. Should I be the leader who takes the risk, or the one who plays it safe? Should I be the leader who speaks the hard truth, or the one who keeps the peace? Should I be the leader who makes the unpopular call, or the one who waits for consensus?

That internal negotiation is exhausting. And under pressure, when cortisol is elevated and cognitive resources are limited, it's paralyzing. The leader doesn't freeze because the decision is complex. They freeze because they don't know who they are in relation to the decision.

I watched this pattern play out with a CEO I coached — a founder who had grown a company to $150 million in revenue. He needed to make a call on accelerating a new product line. The data was only sixty percent complete. His marketing team said wait. His finance team said go. The board wanted decisiveness. And in that compression, he chose speed — not because speed was the right call, but because his survival brain told him that hesitation would look like weakness to investors.

He wasn't deciding from strategy. He was deciding from fear — fear of how he'd be perceived if he slowed down. And within a quarter, the missing data would have changed the decision entirely.

When we unpacked that moment, the real issue wasn't data or timing. It was identity. He had never clearly defined for himself the difference between decisive leadership and reactive speed. His identity under pressure defaulted to *fast means strong, slow means weak.* And that unexamined belief cost him a quarter, credibility, and the trust of a team that needed something better than speed disguised as conviction.

Conviction doesn't mean you're sure you're right. It means you're sure you're deciding for the right reasons.

The Four Decision Traps Under Pressure

When identity isn't anchored, pressure pushes leaders into one of four decision traps. You'll recognize them. You may have lived in them.

The Approval Trap

The leader makes the decision that will generate the least resistance. They poll the room, read the politics, and choose the path that keeps the most people comfortable. It looks like consensus-building. It's actually fear of disapproval driving the call. The cost: the decision that needed to be made — the one that was right but uncomfortable — doesn't get made. And the team learns that comfort outranks clarity.

The Speed Trap

The leader decides fast to relieve the pressure of uncertainty. Any decision feels better than the discomfort of sitting in ambiguity. It looks decisive. It's actually the nervous system's need for resolution overriding the brain's need for clarity. The cost: premature commitments, reversed decisions, and a team that can't trust the leader's calls because they change too often.

The Perfection Trap

The leader waits for complete data, perfect conditions, or certainty before moving. They request more analysis, schedule more meetings, commission more reports. It looks like thoroughness. It's actually fear of being wrong wearing the mask of rigor. The cost: decisions get made by default — by delay, by inaction, by the market moving while the leader stands still.

The Isolation Trap

The leader makes the decision alone, without input, without collaboration, without the perspectives that would sharpen the call. It looks like ownership. It's actually the Controller default from Chapter 4 — the belief that *if I don't do this myself, it won't get done right.* The cost: the team feels bypassed, the decision lacks the intelligence of multiple perspectives, and the leader carries a weight that was never theirs to carry alone.

All four traps have something in common: the leader isn't deciding from their values. They're deciding from their fear. And fear under pressure is a terrible decision-making framework. It optimizes for emotional relief, not leadership integrity.

The Decision Protocol: The Values Filter

This is the practical tool for the third move. Once you've regulated your state and reframed the situation from threat to challenge, you run the Decision Protocol. It's built on a single principle: under pressure, your identity and values must be the anchor for your decisions, not the circumstances, the politics, or the emotional weather of the room.

The protocol has four steps.

Step One: Name What's Pulling You

Before you decide anything, name the forces pulling at the decision. Externally and internally.

Externally: Who wants what? What's the political landscape? Where is the pressure to decide fast, to decide safely, to decide a certain way?

Internally: What is your nervous system pulling you toward? What trap are you closest to — Approval, Speed, Perfection, or Isolation? What does your survival brain want you to do?

Name it all. On paper if you can. In your head if you must. The naming separates you from the pull. It gives you the observer position that regulation opened up — now applied specifically to the decision.

Step Two: Run the Values Filter

This is the core of the protocol. Ask three questions, in sequence:

> **Clarity** — What would the leader I'm becoming choose here? Not the leader I've been. Not the leader my survival brain defaults to. The

one I'm building — the identity I named in the Pressure Reflection of Chapter 4.

Integrity — Does this decision align with the values I've stated publicly as a leader? If my team could see the internal process behind this decision — the real reasons, not the stated reasons — would they trust it?

Sustainability — Can I stand behind this decision in six months? Not just defend it — stand behind it. Will this decision still feel right when the pressure has passed and the full consequences have played out?

These three filters — Clarity, Integrity, Sustainability — do something that no amount of data or analysis can do: they anchor the decision in who you are, not in what the pressure is telling you to do. And decisions anchored in identity hold under heat. Decisions anchored in fear break the moment the pressure shifts.

Step Three: Decide With Conviction, Not Certainty

This distinction is everything.

Most leaders believe they need certainty before they can decide. They need to know the decision is right. They need a guarantee of the outcome. They need the data to be complete, the stakeholders to be aligned, and the risk to be contained.

That's not how high-pressure decisions work. High-pressure decisions, by definition, involve incomplete data, competing stakeholders, and uncontainable risk. Waiting for certainty is the Perfection Trap. It's not rigor. It's avoidance.

What you need is not certainty. What you need is conviction — the ability to commit to a decision because it's aligned with your identity and values, even when the outcome is uncertain.

Conviction doesn't mean you're sure you're right. It means you're sure you're *deciding for the right reasons.* And a leader who decides with conviction — who can say clearly, "This is what I believe is right, and here's why" — earns more trust than a leader who makes the objectively correct call but can't explain the reasoning behind it.

Because teams don't follow decisions. They follow leaders. And they follow leaders who know who they are.

Step Four: Communicate the Decision as Identity, Not Just Strategy

This is the step most leaders skip, and it's the one that determines whether the decision builds trust or erodes it.

When you communicate a high-pressure decision, don't just communicate the what and the why. Communicate the *who.* Let the team see the identity behind the decision.

"We're making this call because it aligns with who we are as a team and what we've committed to building. It's not the easiest path, but it's the one I can stand behind — and I'm asking you to stand with me."

That's different from: "After careful analysis, we've decided to pursue Option B based on the projected ROI."

Both are legitimate. But the first one earns commitment. The second earns compliance. Under pressure, when the execution gets hard and the team needs to push through discomfort, the difference between commitment and compliance is the difference between a decision that holds and one that quietly dies.

Decisions in Practice: Three Scenarios

The Hire That Doesn't Feel Right

You're filling a critical leadership role. The top candidate checks every box on paper — experience, track record, references. But something doesn't sit right.

The interviews went well, but your gut is uneasy. Your team is pushing to move fast because the gap is hurting.

The Approval Trap says: hire them, the team needs it. The Speed Trap says: close it now, the gap is costing you. Your nervous system wants the relief of resolution.

You run the Values Filter.

Clarity: The leader I'm becoming doesn't fill a role to relieve pressure. They fill a role to build the team. If this person doesn't feel right, there's a reason — and ignoring it to move fast is a pattern I'm leaving behind.

Integrity: If my team could see the internal process — that I had doubts and hired anyway to relieve my own discomfort — they wouldn't trust it.

Sustainability: In six months, will I stand behind this hire, or will I be managing the consequences of a decision I made from pressure instead of clarity?

You extend the search. It takes three more weeks. The right hire shows up. And the team, who initially pushed for speed, sees a leader who doesn't make critical calls out of desperation.

The Tough Conversation That Can't Wait Anymore

A senior leader on your team has been underperforming for months. Everyone sees it. The data supports it. But the conversation keeps getting postponed because the emotional cost feels too high. This person was here in the early days. They're loyal. Letting them go — or even confronting the performance gap directly — feels like a betrayal.

The Approval Trap says: give them another quarter. The Perfection Trap says: gather more documentation first. Your Avoider default says: the timing isn't right.

You run the Values Filter.

Clarity: The leader I'm becoming has difficult conversations when they're needed, not when they're convenient. Delay is not loyalty. It's avoidance. And my avoidance is costing the rest of the team.

Integrity: If my team could see that I've been avoiding this conversation for months because of my own discomfort, they wouldn't see loyalty. They'd see a leader who protects relationships over standards.

Sustainability: In six months, I want to look back and know I handled this with directness and respect — not that I waited until the damage was irreversible.

You schedule the conversation. You prepare it with the same rigor you'd bring to any strategic initiative. You lead it anchored in identity: *I'm the leader who tells the truth with respect, not the one who avoids it with good intentions.* The conversation is hard. But the message it sends to the rest of the organization is worth more than a hundred values statements: performance matters here, and so does how we hold each other accountable.

The Strategic Pivot Everyone Else Is Resisting

You see a shift in the market that your executive team doesn't see yet — or doesn't want to see. The data is emerging, not definitive. The current strategy is working, but you believe it has a shelf life. Pivoting now means disrupting something that's functional in service of something that's uncertain.

The Approval Trap says: wait until the team sees it too. The Perfection Trap says: wait until the data is conclusive. The room wants to stay the course.

You run the Values Filter.

Clarity: The leader I'm becoming sees around corners and has the courage to act on what they see, even when the room isn't ready. Leading means going first. That's the job.

Integrity: If I wait for consensus and the market shifts the way I believe it will, I'll have chosen comfort over conviction. My team deserves a leader who moves with vision, not one who waits for permission.

Sustainability: In six months, do I want to be the leader who saw the shift and moved, or the one who saw it and waited until it was too late to be strategic?

You make the case. Not from panic, not from ego, but from a clear, regulated, reframed position of conviction. You bring the team into the reasoning. You show them the data, name the uncertainty, and tell them what you believe and why. Some will disagree. That's fine. Alignment doesn't require agreement. It requires a leader who has the clarity to make the call and the integrity to own it.

Teams don't follow decisions. They follow leaders. And they follow leaders who know who they are.

The Condition Underneath: Identity Clarity

In Chapter 5, I introduced the three internal conditions that make the Pressure Performance System sustainable: Identity Clarity, Emotional Regulation, and Execution Discipline. Each condition sits underneath a specific part of the system.

Identity Clarity is the condition underneath Decide.

Emotional Regulation is the condition underneath both Regulate and Reframe — it gives you the state to think clearly, and the steadiness to see the situation as a challenge instead of a threat. Reframing gives you the lens to see accurately. But the *quality* of the decision you make — whether it holds under sustained pressure, whether it earns trust, whether it builds the culture you're trying to create — depends entirely on how clear you are about who you are.

This is why the pressure profile work in Chapter 4 matters so much. When you've identified your dominant default, your primary pressure arena, and the belief underneath your pattern, you've done the foundational work of identity clarity. You know where your decision-making breaks down. You know which trap you're most likely to fall into. And you know the story your survival brain tells that makes the trap feel like wisdom.

The Values Filter only works when you have values to filter through. And those values — the ones that actually hold under pressure, not the ones on your company's wall — come from identity work. From asking the questions: Who am I when the pressure strips everything else away? What do I stand for when standing for something that costs me something? What kind of leader am I building, and does this decision serve that person?

Identity Clarity is not something you achieve once. It's something you deepen every time you face a hard decision and choose from your values instead of your fear. Every time you run the Values Filter and make the call that's aligned instead of the one that's easy, your identity as that kind of leader gets stronger. The decision builds the identity. The identity builds the next decision. It's a cycle. And over time, it becomes the most powerful leadership asset you own.

What's Ahead

You now have three moves. Regulating gives you access to your thinking brain. Reframe gives you the lens to see the situation as a challenge instead of a threat. Deciding gives you the anchor to choose from identity and values instead of fear and pressure.

There's one move left. And it's the one where everything gets tested.

Because the best decision in the world means nothing if it doesn't get executed. And under pressure, execution is where most leaders lose their nerve. They make the right call in the meeting and then soften it in the hallway. They commit to the hard path and then quietly take the easy one when no one's watching. They decide with conviction and then fail to follow through with discipline.

In the next chapter, we build the fourth and final move: Execute. Because the gap between the decision and the delivery is where pressure reveals one more thing about who you are.

And that gap is closeable.

Pressure Reflection: Chapter 8

These questions are designed to sharpen your decision-making identity. Use a real decision you're facing right now.

Question One:

What is the most significant decision you're currently avoiding, delaying, or struggling with? Name it clearly. Not the situation around it — the actual decision that needs to be made.

Question Two:

Which of the four decision traps is pulling you? Approval, Speed, Perfection, or Isolation? Be honest about the force underneath your delay or your impulse. What is your survival brain trying to protect you from?

Question Three:

Run the Values Filter. *Clarity:* What would the leader you're becoming choose? *Integrity:* If your team could see the real reasons behind your process, would they trust it? *Sustainability:* Will you stand behind this decision in six months?

Question Four:

What is the identity cost of making the right decision? What story about yourself do you have to let go of in order to make the call that's aligned? Name it. That story is usually the thing standing between you and the decision.

Question Five:

If you make this decision from conviction — not certainty, but conviction — how will you communicate it? Write the first three sentences you'd say to your team. Lead with identity, not just strategy. Let them see the *who* behind the *what.*

Question Six:

What is one decision you made in the past from a survival trap that you now wish you'd made from your values? What would have been different — not just in the outcome, but in who you became as a result? Let that inform the decision in front of you now.

In the next chapter, we complete the system with the fourth move — Execute — because a decision without follow-through is just an intention. And pressure doesn't reward intentions. It rewards discipline.

"Conviction doesn't mean you're sure you're right. It means you're sure you're deciding for the right reasons."

— *Elevate Under Pressure*, Chapter 8

9

EXECUTE — FOLLOW THROUGH WITH DISCIPLINE. DELIVER UNDER PRESSURE.

I want to tell you about mile twenty-six of my first (and last) ultramarathon.

Not mile one, where the energy is high and the legs are fresh and the decision to run a 50k feels like the most inspiring thing you've ever done. Not mile ten, where the training kicks in and the body settles into rhythm. Not even mile twenty, where the discomfort is real but the finish is mathematically possible and the mind still has something left.

Mile twenty-six. Where the decision to keep running has nothing to do with inspiration, adrenaline, or even stubbornness. Where your body has stopped cooperating. Where your brain is generating a continuous, persuasive argument for why stopping is the rational choice. Where every aid station looks like a finish line and every volunteer's face says what your survival brain is screaming: *You've done enough. You can stop.*

That's the execution gap. Not the start. Not the decision. The long, unglamorous middle where the follow-through either holds or it doesn't.

I've completed ultramarathons. I've also dropped out of them. And the difference between the two was never fitness. It was never the quality of the decision at mile zero. It was whether I had the execution discipline to keep moving when the initial energy was gone, the pain was real, and the only thing left was the commitment I'd made to myself before the pressure arrived.

Leadership under pressure works exactly the same way.

The Execution Gap

By now, you have three moves working. Regulating gives you access to your thinking brain. Reframe shifts your interpretation from threat to challenge. Decide anchors your choice in identity and values.

All of that can happen in thirty seconds. And all of it can unravel in the hours, days, and weeks that follow if you don't have the fourth move.

The execution gap is the space between the decision and the delivery. Between the commitment made in the meeting and the follow-through required after it. Between the call you know is right and the sustained discipline to hold the line when the resistance comes — and the resistance always comes.

This is where most leaders lose. Not because they made the wrong decision. Not because they lacked clarity or composure. But because the energy of the decision faded, the pressure of maintaining it mounted, and they quietly softened the commitment without anyone noticing — least of all themselves.

I've watched it happen hundreds of times in my coaching work.

The executive who makes a bold strategic pivot in the quarterly meeting and then, three weeks later, starts making exceptions that undermine the pivot because the pushback from the team is wearing him down.

The founder who commits to letting go of a senior leader and then postpones the conversation twice, redefines the timeline, and eventually restructures the role instead of having the direct conversation.

The leader who establishes new performance standards with conviction and then, when the first high performer pushes back, quietly lowers the standard to avoid the conflict.

In each case, the decision was right. The regulation was clean. The reframe was accurate. The values filter was run. But the execution didn't hold. And the cost of a good decision with poor execution is worse than no decision at all — because the team saw the commitment and then watched it erode. That erosion doesn't just cost the specific initiative. It costs the leader's credibility.

Because here's what your team learns when you don't follow through: *What this leader says under pressure doesn't hold. Wait long enough and the standard will soften.* Once that belief takes root in your culture, it takes years to undo.

What Execution Discipline Actually Is

Execution discipline is not willpower. That's the first thing I need you to understand, because the willpower model of execution is the reason most leaders fail at it.

Willpower is a depletable resource. Under normal conditions, it's limited. Under pressure — when cortisol is elevated, when cognitive load is high, when emotional energy is being spent on regulation and reframing and decision-making — willpower is nearly nonexistent. If your execution strategy depends on waking up every morning and muscling through the follow-through, you will fail. Not because you're weak. Because you're human.

Execution discipline is systems. It's the structures, rhythms, and accountability architectures that carry the execution forward regardless of how you feel on any given day. It's the difference between a leader who performs when motivated and a leader who delivers consistently — especially when motivation is gone.

In the kitchen, we didn't execute under pressure because we were inspired. We executed because the system demanded it. The ticket rail. The timing of the courses. The call-and-response between the pass and the stations. The prep lists that were done before service, every day, without exception, because the system didn't care whether you felt like doing prep. The guests were coming at six. The system held when the person wavered.

That's what I want to build for your leadership. Not more motivation. More systems.

A decision without follow-through is just an intention. And pressure doesn't reward intentions. It rewards discipline.

The Three Ways Execution Fails Under Pressure

Before I give you the tools, I want to name the three specific ways execution breaks down under sustained pressure. Understanding these helps you see where your system needs reinforcement.

The Standard Softens

This is the most common and the most invisible. The leader sets a clear standard — in a meeting, in a memo, in a strategic commitment. Then, as the weeks pass and the pressure of maintaining that standard builds, exceptions start appearing. Small ones at first. A deadline that slides a few days. A performance expectation that gets reinterpreted. A behavior that gets overlooked because addressing it feels like more than the leader has energy for.

Each individual exception looks reasonable. In aggregate, they dismantle the standard entirely. And the leader never made a conscious decision to lower the bar. The bar just drifted down because there was no system to hold it.

The Conversation Doesn't Happen

Every significant execution requires follow-through conversations. The check-in after the hard decision. The accountability conversation when someone isn't delivering. The reinforcement conversation when the team needs to hear the commitment restated in the face of resistance.

Under pressure, these conversations are the first things to go. Not because the leader forgets. Because the emotional cost of each conversation adds up, and without a system that schedules and protects them, they get crowded out by whatever is loudest and most urgent.

The result: decisions get made and never reinforced. Commitments get announced and never followed up. The team learns that the real culture isn't what gets said in the meeting — it's what gets enforced after it.

The Leader Becomes the Bottleneck

This is the Controller default showing up in execution. The leader makes the decision and then can't let go of the implementation. They check every deliverable. They insert themselves into every workstream. They hold the execution so tightly that the team can't move without them.

It looks like ownership. It's actually a failure to build execution systems that extend beyond one person. And the cost is devastating: the leader burns out, the team's capacity atrophies, and the organization's execution speed is permanently limited by one person's bandwidth.

The Execution Protocol: Three Systems That Hold Under Pressure

This is practical architecture. Three systems that, when implemented together, close the execution gap and protect your follow-through under sustained pressure.

System One: The 72-Hour Commitment Window

The single most important execution principle I teach leaders is this: the first seventy-two hours after a decision are where execution lives or dies.

This is when energy is highest and resistance hasn't fully organized. This is when the team is watching most closely to see if the leader's commitment is real. And this is the window where the first visible action establishes the credibility of the decision.

The protocol is simple: within seventy-two hours of any significant decision, complete at least one concrete, visible action that signals the decision is real. Not a plan to act. Not a meeting to discuss next steps. An action.

If you decide to restructure a team, the seventy-two-hour action is the first conversation with the person most affected. If you commit to a strategic pivot, the seventy-two-hour action is the first reallocation of resources — time, budget, or people — that makes the pivot tangible. If you made a performance commitment, the seventy-two-hour action is the first accountability conversation.

The 72-Hour Commitment Window works because of a simple psychological truth: action creates momentum, and momentum sustains execution. But the window closes fast. After seventy-two hours, the energy of the decision fades, competing priorities rush in, and the execution gap opens wide.

Every major decision gets a seventy-two-hour action. Non-negotiable. This single practice has saved more commitments from dying in my clients' organizations than any other tool I've ever taught.

System Two: The Accountability Architecture

Execution under pressure cannot depend on one person's memory, motivation, or willpower. It needs structure. And structure means other people.

The Accountability Architecture has three components:

The Execution Partner — One person — not your entire team, one person — who knows the commitment, knows the timeline, and has explicit permission to ask you about it. This isn't a mentor or a coach. It's a peer or a direct report who serves one function: they close the gap between what you committed to and what you're actually doing. The question they ask is simple: "Did you do what you said you'd do?"

The Rhythm — A recurring touchpoint — weekly at most, biweekly at minimum — where execution gets reviewed. Not the strategy. Not the decision. The execution. What was supposed to happen this week? Did it happen? If not, why — and what needs to change? This rhythm works best when it's short, structured, and protected from cancellation. Fifteen minutes. Same time every week. It doesn't move.

The Public Commitment — The act of stating your commitment in front of the people who will be affected by it. Not as a performance. As a leadership act. When you tell your team, "Here's what I've committed to, here's the timeline, and here's how I'm going to hold myself accountable," you've created a social contract that is significantly harder to break than a private intention. Pressure makes us want to keep commitments private so we can quietly abandon them. Execution discipline makes them public so we can't.

The Accountability Architecture doesn't replace your internal discipline. It reinforces it. It creates the external structure that holds you to your own standards when the internal pressure to soften is strongest.

System Three: The Standard-Protection Protocol

This is the system that prevents the invisible drift I described earlier — the slow softening of standards that dismantles execution without a single conscious decision.

The protocol works like this: when you set a standard, you simultaneously define the first exception that will test it. Not if. When. Because it's coming.

If you've set a new meeting culture standard — meetings start on time, agendas required, decisions documented — then define in advance: what will I do the first time a senior leader shows up late? What will I do the first time someone skips the agenda? What will I do the first time a decision doesn't get documented?

If you've committed to a performance standard — no more quiet acceptance of missed targets — then define: what will I do the first time my strongest performer misses? Because that's the real test. Holding the standard for underperformers is easy. Holding it for your best people is where execution discipline lives.

The Standard-Protection Protocol is simply this: **decide how you'll respond to the first violation before it happens.** Because in the moment, under pressure, with the relationship cost right in front of you, your survival brain will generate a convincing argument for making an exception. If you've already decided your response, you don't need willpower. You need memory.

Pre-decided responses hold under pressure. In-the-moment negotiations with yourself do not.

Execution in Practice: The Restructure That Required Six Months of Holding the Line

Let me give you one extended scenario instead of three short ones, because execution is not a single moment. Execution is sustained discipline over time. And the real test of this move is whether you can hold it long after the energy of the decision has faded.

I coached a COO through a major organizational restructure. The decision was sound — she'd regulated, reframed, run the Values Filter, and committed to a redesign that would eliminate a redundant management layer, redeploy resources to growth initiatives, and promote three high-potential leaders into expanded roles.

The restructure was announced well. The team understood the why. The initial energy was strong.

Then week three hit.

One of the displaced managers — a well-liked, long-tenured leader — began campaigning quietly against the changes. Not publicly. In hallway conversations, one-on-ones, and carefully worded Slack messages. The mood shifted. Two of the three promoted leaders started second-guessing whether they'd been set up to fail. The COO's own boss asked whether the timing was right.

This is where execution dies. Not in the decision. In week three. In the slow accumulation of resistance that makes the leader question whether the cost of continuing is worth it.

Here's what held.

The **72-Hour Commitment Window** had already been executed. In the first three days after announcing the restructure, the COO had the hardest conversation first — directly with the displaced manager. She didn't wait for him to campaign. She sat with him, acknowledged the difficulty, was direct about the decision, and outlined his transition support. That early action established credibility.

The **Accountability Architecture** was in place. Her execution partner — her CHRO — checked in every Monday for fifteen minutes. Not on the strategy. On the execution. *Did you have the conversation with the promoted leaders this week? Did you address the resistance directly? Did the resource reallocation happen on schedule?* Every week. Same time. Didn't move.

The **Standard-Protection Protocol** had been defined before the announcement. She had already decided: if someone campaigns against the restructure behind closed doors, I address it directly within forty-eight hours. When it happened, she didn't negotiate with herself about whether to let it slide. She'd already decided. She had the conversation.

Six months later, the restructure was complete. The three promoted leaders were performing. The organization had shed a layer of management that had been slowing it down for years. And the COO had established something no single decision could have built: a reputation for follow-through under sustained pressure.

That reputation is worth more than any strategic insight. Because teams don't trust strategies. They trust leaders who do what they say they're going to do, especially when it gets hard.

The cost of a good decision with poor execution is worse than no decision at all.

The Condition Underneath: Execution Discipline

Execution Discipline is the third internal condition of the Pressure Performance System. Identity Clarity stabilizes your decisions. Emotional Regulation stabilizes your state. Execution Discipline stabilizes your follow-through.

And like the other two conditions, it's not a skill you learn once. It's a capacity you build through repetition and commitment.

Every time you honor the 72-Hour Commitment Window, your execution discipline gets stronger. Every time you show up for the accountability rhythm even when you'd rather skip it, it gets stronger. Every time you hold the standard when the pressure to soften is real, it gets stronger.

And over time, something shifts. Execution stops being the thing you have to *force* and becomes the thing you simply *do*. The follow-through becomes part of your identity. You become the leader whose commitments hold — not because you're grinding, but because your systems carry the weight that willpower can't.

This is the final piece of the infrastructure. Identity Clarity, Emotional Regulation, Execution Discipline. Three conditions that make the four moves sustainable. Without them, the system is a set of techniques. With them, the system is who you are.

The Complete System

Let me give you the full picture one more time, because this is the last chapter of Part Two and this is the architecture you're taking into the rest of the book and the rest of your leadership.

It builds the internal conditions of Identity Clarity, Emotional Regulation, and Execution Discipline — and activates them in real time through four moves: Regulate, Reframe, Decide, and Execute.

Regulate: Choose your state before you choose your response. Tool: the Regulation Protocol — Name It, Slow It, Choose It.

Reframe: Shift from threat to challenge. Tool: the Reframe Protocol — What's actually at stake? Where's the leadership opportunity? Who do I want to be on the other side of this?

Decide: Anchor in identity and values. Move with clarity. Tool: the Values Filter — Clarity, Integrity, Sustainability.

Execute: Follow through with discipline. Deliver under pressure. Tools: the 72-Hour Commitment Window, the Accountability Architecture, the Standard-Protection Protocol.

Four moves. Three conditions. One system. Built for the moments that matter most.

What's Ahead

Part Two is complete. You have the system.

In Part Three, we take it further. Because the Pressure Performance System doesn't stop with personal mastery. The leaders who transform organizations don't just regulate, reframe, decide, and execute for themselves. They build cultures where everyone around them can do the same.

In Chapter 10, we'll explore what happens when a leader's regulated presence becomes the culture — and how to build a team, an organization, and a legacy that elevates under pressure, not just a leader who does.

And in Chapter 11, we'll come back to where we started: identity. Because the final transformation isn't about what you do under pressure. It's about who you've become.

Pressure Reflection: Chapter 9

These questions are designed to expose where your execution breaks down and build the systems to hold it.

Question One:

Think about the last significant commitment you made as a leader that didn't hold. Not a decision that was wrong — a decision that was right but didn't get executed. What happened? Where in the execution gap did it break down? Did the standard soften, the conversation not happen, or did you become the bottleneck?

Question Two:

What is the decision you made most recently that needs the 72-Hour Commitment Window? What is the one concrete, visible action you can take in the next seventy-two hours that will signal the decision is real — to your team and to yourself?

Question Three:

Who is your Execution Partner? Name them. If you don't have one, identify who it should be. What is the conversation you need to have with them to establish the accountability rhythm? Schedule it.

Question Four:

What is the standard you've set that is most at risk of softening right now? Name the first exception that's going to test it. Now decide — in advance, right now, before the pressure arrives — how you'll respond. Write it down. That pre-decided response is your Standard-Protection Protocol.

Question Five:

Be honest: where is willpower still your primary execution strategy? Where are you grinding through follow-through instead of building systems to carry it? What would change if you replaced willpower with the Accountability Architecture in that specific area?

Question Six:

Look at the complete system — Regulate, Reframe, Decide, Execute. Which move is your strongest? Which is your weakest? The strongest is your leadership advantage under pressure. The weakest is where the next level of your performance lives. Both matter. Name them.

In Part Three, we take the system beyond yourself. Because the ultimate measure of a leader under pressure isn't how they perform. It's what they build.

"A decision without follow-through is just an intention. And pressure doesn't reward intentions. It rewards discipline."

— *Elevate Under Pressure*, Chapter 9

PART THREE
THE ELEVATED LEADER

10
BUILDING A CULTURE THAT ELEVATES UNDER PRESSURE

When I served as Chief People Officer, I learned something about leadership culture that no business book had prepared me for.

We had a strong executive team. Good people. Experienced operators. Individually, most of them performed well. But under organizational pressure — a restructure, a market shift, a quarter where everything tightened at once — the culture fractured. Not visibly. Not dramatically. It fractured in the space between the executive floor and the people doing the work.

The senior leaders would make decisions in the room and then fail to carry them consistently to their teams. Not out of negligence. Out of pressure. Each leader was managing their own nervous system, their own defaults, their own survival patterns — and under enough heat, those patterns leaked. The

Controller tightened. The Avoider deferred. The Reactor sharpened. The Disconnector went quiet. And every one of those defaults sent a signal to the next layer of leadership that cascaded through the organization.

The company didn't have a strategy problem. It had a pressure culture problem. The leaders at the top were individually capable, but their unregulated responses under pressure had become the organization's operating system. Not the strategy on the wall. Not the values in the handbook. The actual way people experienced leadership when things got hard.

That experience changed how I think about the Pressure Performance System. Because the system doesn't stop with you. It can't. Your regulation — or your dysregulation — becomes your team's reality. Your reframe — or your threat response — becomes the narrative the organization runs. Your execution discipline — or your softening under resistance — becomes the standard your culture enforces.

You are not just leading under pressure. You are building the culture that determines how everyone around you performs under pressure.

That's what this chapter is about.

Your State Becomes the Room's State

I said this in Chapter 6, and I want to go deeper here because it's the single most important principle in organizational pressure leadership:

Your regulation is contagious. So is your dysregulation.

This isn't a metaphor. It's neuroscience. Mirror neurons — the neural circuits that fire in response to observing someone else's state — mean that the people in your room are literally co-regulating with you. When you walk into a meeting regulated, present, and composed, the room's collective nervous system calms. People think more clearly. They contribute more openly. They access their best thinking instead of their survival defaults.

When you walk in dysregulated — sharp, tense, rushed, distracted — the room's collective nervous system activates. Threat spreads. People go quiet, go defensive, or go performative. The quality of thinking in the room drops. Not because the people changed. Because the leader's state changed the conditions.

This is why I call psychological safety a regulation issue, not a policy issue. Every leader I've ever coached wants their team to speak up, challenge ideas, bring the hard truths. But psychological safety doesn't come from telling people it's safe to speak. It comes from the leader's nervous system making it safe. When you can hold challenge without reacting, hear bad news without punishing, and sit in disagreement without escalating — your team learns that the room is safe. Not because you said so. Because they *felt* it.

And they felt it because you were regulated.

The reverse is equally true. If you say the room is safe but your tone sharpens the moment someone pushes back, the room learns the opposite lesson — and learns it permanently. One dysregulated response from a senior leader can undo months of cultural messaging about openness and trust. Because the body believes the leader's state, not the leader's words.

This is the multiplier effect of the Pressure Performance System. When you regulate, you don't just change your performance. You change the conditions for everyone around you to perform. That's not an incremental leadership improvement. That's a cultural transformation.

You are not just leading under pressure. You are building the culture that determines how everyone around you performs under pressure.

The Cascade Problem: How Pressure Defaults Spread

In my CPO role, I watched something happen that every organizational leader needs to understand: pressure defaults don't stay with the leader who has them. They cascade.

When a senior leader operates from a Controller default under pressure, their direct reports learn that the organization rewards control. They start tightening their own grip on their teams. Within two layers, autonomy has evaporated and the organization's decision-making speed has collapsed — not because of a policy, but because one leader's survival pattern became the management culture.

When a senior leader operates from an Avoider default, their direct reports learn that difficult conversations don't happen here. Performance issues go unaddressed. Underperformers stay in role. High performers watch, calculate, and quietly leave. Within a year, the organization has a retention problem it can't explain and a performance standard no one believes in.

When a senior leader operates from a Reactor default, their direct reports learn that the organization runs on adrenaline and urgency. Everything becomes a fire drill. Speed replaces strategy. Burnout becomes the norm, and the people who thrive in chaos get promoted while the steady, strategic operators get marginalized.

When a senior leader operates from a Disconnector default, their direct reports learn that information doesn't flow here. Communication stops. Silos form. Teams operate in isolation, building redundant capabilities and working from assumptions instead of shared intelligence.

In every case, the leader didn't intend to create that culture. They didn't design it. Their pressure default designed it for them. And by the time the pattern is visible at the organizational level, it's been running for years.

This is why the Pressure Performance System matters beyond the individual. It's not just about how you perform under pressure. It's about what your performance under pressure is building in the people around you. Every time you regulate in front of your team, you're teaching them that regulation is possible. Every time you reframe publicly, you're showing them how to interpret pressure differently. Every time you decide from values and execute with discipline, you're modeling the leadership identity you want them to develop.

You're not just using the system. You're transmitting it.

Equipping Your Next Layer: The Succession Depth Problem

Here's the organizational pressure point I see most consistently in mid-market companies that have grown fast: the top leader is carrying everything, and the next layer isn't ready.

Not because the talent isn't there. The talent is almost always there. It's because no one has been developed to lead under pressure. The organization has built executors — people who can deliver on direction, manage projects, and hit targets when conditions are favorable — but not leaders who can regulate their own nervous systems, reframe high-stakes situations, make identity-anchored decisions, and follow through under sustained resistance.

That gap is what I call the succession depth problem. And it's the most expensive vulnerability in mid-market organizations today. Because the moment the senior leader can't be in the room — due to illness, transition, burnout, or simply being in a different meeting — the organization's capacity to perform under pressure drops to whatever the next layer can hold.

The Pressure Performance System solves this. Not by identifying successors on a chart, but by building the actual capacity to lead under pressure in the people who will need it.

Here's how.

Teach the Language

The first step is making the system visible. Give your next layer the vocabulary: Regulate, Reframe, Decide, Execute. Name the four defaults. Name the three conditions. When your team has shared language for what happens under pressure, they can see their own patterns and each other's patterns without shame, without blame, and without the protective silence that usually surrounds pressure behavior.

I've watched leadership teams transform the moment they had shared language for their pressure dynamics. Instead of *Why does she always go quiet in those meetings?* the conversation becomes *She's in a Disconnector default right now. What does she need to regulate?* That shift — from judgment to diagnosis — changes everything about how a team holds each other under pressure.

Model It Publicly

Your next layer won't learn the system from training. They'll learn it from watching you. And that means you need to make your regulation visible. Not performatively. Authentically.

When you catch yourself in a survival response, name it out loud: "I just noticed I'm reacting to this instead of leading through it. Give me a moment." When you reframe in a meeting, make the shift transparent: "The numbers feel like a threat, but what's the actual leadership opportunity here?" When you make a tough call, share the Values Filter: "I made this decision because it aligns with who we are as a team, even though it's not the easiest path."

Every time you do this, you're giving your next layer a live demonstration of the system working in real conditions. That's more powerful than any workshop.

Create Pressure Reps

You develop leaders who can perform under pressure the same way you develop any high-performance skill: through deliberate, structured repetition in progressively challenging conditions.

Put your next-layer leaders in high-stakes situations with support. Let them lead the difficult conversation while you observe and debrief. Let them present to the board while you sit in the back of the room. Let them make the call on a significant decision while you hold the safety net. Then debrief using the system language: *Where did you regulate? Where did the survival brain take over? What was your reframe? What did the Values Filter tell you?*

These pressure reps are how capacity gets built. Not through theory. Through experience, with language, with feedback, with a system that gives the experience a structure the leader can learn from.

Build the Accountability Architecture Across the Team

The same Accountability Architecture from Chapter 9 works at the team level. Execution Partners become peer accountability pairs. The Rhythm becomes a team cadence where execution gets reviewed collectively. Public Commitments become team commitments that everyone can see and hold.

When the Accountability Architecture extends beyond you, the execution discipline becomes organizational — not dependent on your presence. And that's the real test of succession depth: can this team hold the standard, make the decision, and follow through when you're not in the room?

The Pressure Culture Audit: Five Questions That Reveal Your Organization's Real Culture

Culture isn't what you put on the wall. Culture is what happens under pressure when no one is scripting the behavior. If you want to know what your organization's culture actually is, these five questions will tell you.

One: What happens to decision speed under pressure?

Does the organization make faster, clearer decisions — or does it freeze? If decisions slow under pressure, the organization is running a collective Avoider or Perfection default. If decisions accelerate without rigor, it's running a collective Reactor default.

Two: What happens to communication under pressure?

Does information flow more freely when the stakes are high — or does it contract? Do silos deepen? Does the leadership team go quiet? If communication contracts under pressure, the organization lacks the regulation infrastructure to keep the thinking brain online across layers.

Three: What happens to accountability under pressure?

Do standards hold — or do exceptions multiply? When the quarter gets hard, does the organization tighten its standards or soften them? The answer reveals whether execution discipline is individual or systemic.

Four: What happens to the next layer under pressure?

Do your mid-level leaders step up — or wait for direction? When pressure hits, does the organization's capacity expand because more people are leading, or contract because everyone is looking up? The answer reveals your actual succession depth.

Five: What do your best people do under sustained pressure?

Do they lean in — or start leaving? High performers are the earliest indicator of pressure culture health. If your best people are updating their resumes during a tough quarter, the culture isn't giving them what they need to stay: psychological safety, clear direction, and a leader they trust to hold the line.

Answer these five questions honestly and you'll have a more accurate picture of your organizational culture than any engagement survey can give you. And you'll know exactly where the Pressure Performance System needs to extend beyond your own leadership.

Culture isn't what you put on the wall. Culture is what happens under pressure when no one is scripting the behavior.

The Shift: From Personal Mastery to Organizational Architecture

There's a transition point in every leader's development where the question changes.

It starts as: *How do I perform under pressure?*

It becomes: *How do I build an organization that performs under pressure?*

That shift is the difference between a strong individual leader and a leader who builds something that lasts. Because an organization built on one person's capacity to perform under pressure is fragile. It only works when that person is present, regulated, and available. The moment they're not — and that moment will come — the organization's performance drops to whatever the next layer can hold.

The leaders who build lasting organizations don't just use the Pressure Performance System. They install it. They build the language, the practices, the accountability structures, and the development pathways that let the system live in the culture, not just in one person.

That's what you're building now. Not just a better you under pressure. A better organization under pressure. A team that can regulate when the room gets tense. A leadership layer that can reframe a crisis as a challenge without waiting for the CEO to do it for them. A culture where decisions get made from values, not fear. An execution standard that holds because the system holds it, not because one leader is grinding.

This is the work that outlasts you. This is the work that builds legacy. And it starts with the same thing it started with in Chapter 1: seeing clearly what pressure reveals about who you are — and then choosing, deliberately, who you want to be.

Not just for yourself anymore. For everyone who follows your lead.

What's Ahead

In the final chapter, we come home.

Chapter 11 isn't about new tools or new frameworks. It's about the identity transformation that happens when a leader integrates this system so deeply that it's no longer something they do — it's who they are. It's the chapter where the four moves and the three conditions stop being practices and start being identity. Where the Pressure Performance System becomes invisible because it's become you.

We started this book with a question: *Who are you when pressure hits?*

We end it with a different one: *Who have you become?*

Pressure Reflection: Chapter 10

These questions shift the lens from your own performance to the performance culture you're building.

Question One:

Run the Pressure Culture Audit on your own organization or team. Answer all five questions honestly. Where does your culture perform well under pressure, and where does it fracture? Be specific. The fracture points will tell you where your leadership defaults are cascading.

Question Two:

Think about the last time your team was under significant pressure. What was the room's state? Was it regulated or reactive? Calm or tense? Now ask honestly: was that state a reflection of your own? What would have been different in the room if your state had been different?

Question Three:

Who is your next layer? Name the two or three people who would need to lead if you weren't available. How would they perform under the specific kinds of pressure your organization faces? Where are they strong, and where do they default? Can you name their pressure profiles as clearly as you can name your own?

Question Four:

What is one element of the Pressure Performance System you could begin teaching your team this month? The four moves? The default language? The Regulation Protocol? Choose one. Introduce it. The moment you give your team shared language for pressure, the culture begins to shift.

Question Five:

Where are you still the bottleneck? Where does your organization's capacity to perform under pressure depend entirely on your presence in the room? That's your most important succession development target. And it's the place where extending the system beyond yourself will create the most organizational value.

Question Six:

What kind of pressure culture are you building — intentionally or not? If someone observed your team under pressure for a month and wrote down what they saw, what would the report say? Is that the culture you want to leave behind? If not, what needs to change — starting with you?

In the final chapter, we return to where we started — identity — and we ask the question that everything in this book has been building toward: Who have you become?

"You are not just leading under pressure. You are building the culture that determines how everyone around you performs under pressure."

— *Elevate Under Pressure*, Chapter 10

11
THE ELEVATED LEADER — WHO YOU BECOME WHEN PRESSURE BECOMES YOUR TEACHER

I want to tell you about a morning.

Not a dramatic one. Not a crisis. Not a defining moment that makes for a good keynote story. Just a morning.

I woke up early, the way I always do now. I took my dog, Mia, to the forest for our morning walk, did my meditation and yoga. My wife was still sleeping. I made coffee. I sat in the quiet and ran through the day ahead — two coaching sessions, a discovery call with a potential enterprise client, a check-in with my wife's care team, and a block of writing time that I'd committed to protecting.

And somewhere in that quiet, I noticed something. I wasn't anxious. I wasn't bracing. I wasn't scanning for threats that day. I was present. The pressure was still there — all of it, every layer, the caregiving, the business, the weight that doesn't take days off. But my relationship to it had changed.

I wasn't managing the pressure anymore. I was leading alongside it.

That shift didn't happen overnight. It didn't happen in a workshop or after a breakthrough coaching session. It happened the way all real transformation happens — gradually, through thousands of small choices, through the accumulated discipline of regulating when I didn't feel like it, reframing when the threat felt real, deciding from my values when my survival brain was screaming, and following through on commitments when every fiber in me wanted to soften.

It happened because the system stopped being something I used and became something I am.

That's what this chapter is about. Not the tools. You have those. Not the framework. You've learned that. This chapter is about the identity transformation that happens when the Pressure Performance System integrates so deeply into who you are that you no longer think about the moves. You just move.

Pressure was never the obstacle. It was always the invitation.

The Integration Point

There's a moment in every leader's journey through this work where something shifts. It's subtle. It doesn't announce itself. But it's unmistakable once you recognize it.

It's the moment you stop *catching* your survival brain and start *leading from* your thinking brain as a default.

In the early stages of the work, regulation is deliberate. You feel the activation, you name it, you slow it, you choose. The Reframe Protocol takes conscious effort. The Values Filter requires you to stop and ask the questions. The 72-Hour Commitment Window is something you have to remember to do.

At the integration point, all of that becomes automatic. Not in the way your old pressure defaults were automatic — unconscious, unexamined, driven by survival. Automatic in the way that a master chef moves on a busy line. You've practiced the moves so many times that they've become part of how your nervous system responds. The regulation happens before the dysregulation fully forms. The reframe is your first interpretation, not your second. The values are the lens you see through, not a filter you apply after the fact.

This is the difference between a leader who has tools and a leader who has *transformed.* And the transformation is not about becoming someone different. It's about becoming more fully yourself — the version of you that pressure has been trying to reveal all along.

The Three Identity Shifts

Across the hundreds of leaders I've coached through the Pressure Performance System, I've observed three specific identity shifts that happen when the work integrates. They don't happen in order. They don't happen on schedule. But they happen consistently, and each one marks a permanent change in how the leader relates to pressure.

The Shift From Reactive to Responsive

This is the first shift, and it's the most visible. The leader who used to fire from their survival brain — sharp emails, defensive meeting tones, premature decisions, hallway venting — becomes the leader who pauses. Not because they're suppressing. Because they genuinely have a gap between stimulus and response that didn't exist before. They've built it. Through thousands of regulation reps, through the daily practice, through the accumulated discipline of choosing their state.

The teams around these leaders describe the shift before the leaders themselves recognize it. *She's different in meetings now. I can't explain it exactly, but the room feels different when she's leading.* What the team is describing is a nervous system that has changed its default. And their nervous systems are responding to it.

The Shift From Threat-Oriented to Challenge-Oriented

This is the shift that changes the leader's relationship to pressure itself. Before the work, pressure was something to survive, contain, or push through. After the integration, pressure becomes information. Signal. Material to work with.

The leader who used to hear bad news and brace now hears bad news and leans in. Not because they enjoy it. Because their brain has been trained to interpret high-stakes situations as challenges that require leadership, not threats that require defense. The survival brain still fires — it always will — but it no longer runs the narrative.

This is the shift that made the most difference in my own life. Caregiving for my wife, managing the complexity of the business, holding the emotional weight of a life that doesn't lighten on schedule — none of that changed. What changed is that I s*to*pped interpreting the pressure as something happening to me and started engaging with it as something happening *through* me. Not as a philosophy. As an actual, felt shift in how my brain processes daily reality.

Pressure became the teacher instead of the test. And when that shift locks in, it's permanent.

The Shift From Performance to Presence

This is the deepest shift, and it's the one that surprises leaders the most.

Before the work, most leaders under pressure are performing. They're projecting confidence they don't feel. They're managing how others perceive them. They're running a version of leadership that looks good from the outside but costs enormous energy on the inside. Every meeting is a performance. Every crisis is a test of performance. And the gap between who they are and who they're pretending to be gets wider under pressure.

After the integration, performance gives way to presence. The leader stops projecting and starts being. They walk into the room as themselves — regulated, clear, grounded, imperfect, and fully present. They don't need to appear confident because they are confident — not in the outcome, but in who they are regardless of the outcome.

This is what people mean when they talk about executive presence, although most people define it wrong. Executive presence is not charisma. It's not polish. It's not the ability to work a room. Executive presence is the quality of being fully yourself under pressure — without performance, without defense, without the survival brain's constant narration about how you're being perceived.

It's the most powerful thing a leader can bring into a room. And it comes from one place: an identity that has been clarified, regulated, and tested under pressure until it holds without effort.

The Mirror, Revisited

In Chapter 1, I told you that pressure is a mirror. That it doesn't break you — it reveals you. And I told you that the mirror is a gift, because you cannot change what you cannot see.

I want to come back to that, because after everything you've built through this book, the mirror shows something different now.

In Chapter 1, when you looked into the mirror, you saw your defaults. Your survival patterns. The version of yourself that pressure had been revealing without your permission or your awareness.

Now, having built the system — having done the work of regulation, reframing, decision-making, execution, and cultural leadership — what does the mirror show?

It shows a leader who knows who they are. Not perfectly. Not completely. But with enough clarity to lead from identity instead of from survival. A leader who can hold the room steady because they've learned to hold themselves steady first. A leader whose decisions come from values and whose follow-through comes from systems. A leader who doesn't need pressure to stop in order to perform — because they've built something inside themselves that pressure can't touch.

That's the elevated leader. Not a leader without pressure. A leader who has learned to let pressure reveal the best of who they are.

The Work That Never Finishes

I want to be honest with you about something, because I think you've earned it by staying with me this far.

This work doesn't end.

There is no point where you are "done" with the Pressure Performance System. No point where regulation becomes unnecessary, where reframing is automatic in every situation, where every decision comes from perfect clarity, where execution never wavers. If someone tells you they've mastered pressure, they either haven't been tested recently or they're not being honest.

What changes is the baseline. The floor rises. The defaults get healthier. The recovery gets faster. The gap between trigger and regulation shrinks from minutes to seconds. The identity that pressure reveals becomes more and more aligned with the identity you're choosing.

But new pressures will come. Pressures you haven't faced yet. Pressures that will find defaults you didn't know you had. And in those moments, you'll need the system again — not because it failed, but because it's designed for exactly this. For the next moment. For the pressure that hasn't arrived yet. For the version of you that's still becoming.

I'm still becoming. At fifty-six, after forty years of pressure in every domain I could find, I am still discovering defaults I didn't know I had. Still learning to regulate in conditions I haven't practiced. Still finding places where my identity needs to deepen before the next level of leadership becomes accessible.

That's not a failure of the system. That's the point of it. The system doesn't promise you a life without pressure. It promises you a life where pressure makes you better, every single time, if you're willing to let it.

Executive presence is the quality of being fully yourself under pressure — without performance, without defense.

The Complete Architecture: One Final Time

Let me give you the full system one last time. Not as a summary. As an anchor you can return to whenever you need it.

Builds the internal conditions of Identity Clarity, Emotional Regulation, and Execution Discipline — and activates them in real time through four moves:

> **Regulate** — Name it. Slow it. Choose your state before you choose your response.

Reframe — Shift from threat to challenge. Lead the narrative.

Decide — Anchor in identity and values. Move with clarity, not reaction.

Execute — Follow through with discipline. Protect standards. Deliver under pressure.

Four moves. Three conditions. One system. Designed for the moments that matter most.

And underneath all of it, one truth that has held from the first page to this one:

Pressure doesn't reveal weakness. It reveals identity. And the leaders who elevate under pressure aren't the ones who have less of it. They're the ones who have learned to let it work for them.

Pressure Reflection: Chapter 11

These are the final reflection questions. They're different from the ones that came before. They're not designed to diagnose or build a specific skill. They're designed to help you see who you've become.

Question One:

Go back to the Pressure Reflection in Chapter 1. You wrote down your last significant pressure moment and what it revealed about you. Reread that. Now ask: has anything shifted? Do you see that moment differently now? Does the pattern it revealed feel as fixed as it did then, or has something opened?

Question Two:

Think about the three identity shifts — Reactive to Responsive, Threat-Oriented to Challenge-Oriented, Performance to Presence. Which shift have you already begun to experience, even slightly? Where do you feel the change starting? Name it. Naming the shift reinforces it.

Question Three:

In Chapter 4, you wrote a sentence about the belief underneath your pressure default. *I believe that…* In the same chapter, you wrote a sentence about the belief you'd replace it with. Reread both. Has the new belief started to feel more real? Has the old one started to lose its grip? That movement — however small — is the identity shift in process.

Question Four:

If someone who has never met you watched you lead under pressure this week, what would they see? Not what you would want them to see. What would they observe about your state, your decisions, your communication, your follow-through? Be honest. That honest picture is your current identity under pressure. And it's the starting point for the next phase of the work.

Question Five:

What is the pressure that's coming next? Not the one you're in now — the one on the horizon. The next decision, the next transition, the next season that's going to test you in ways you haven't been tested yet. Name it. And then answer the question that has been at the heart of this entire book: *Who do you want to be when that pressure arrives?*

Write that person down. That's who you're building now.

The Epilogue follows. It's brief. It's personal. And it's the last thing I want to leave you with.

> ***"Pressure was never the obstacle. It was always the invitation."***
>
> **— *Elevate Under Pressure*, Chapter 11**

EPILOGUE PRESSURE WAS ALWAYS THE POINT

I'm writing this on a quiet morning, I love my slow mornings. The coffee is still warm. The day hasn't started demanding anything from me yet.

In a few minutes, it will. The caregiving will begin. The clients will need me. The business will ask questions I don't have complete answers to. The weight will arrive the way it always does — not dramatically, not with a crash, but with the steady, intimate presence of a life that asks everything of you and doesn't negotiate.

And I'll be ready. Not because I've eliminated the pressure. Not because I've figured out some trick to make it lighter. But because I've spent forty years letting pressure teach me who I am. And I've finally stopped fighting the lesson.

I think about the kitchen sometimes. That sixteen-year-old kid stepping onto a high-end line for the first time, orders flying, heat everywhere, no margin for error. I didn't know what I was learning then. I thought I was learning to cook. I was learning to perform under pressure. I was learning that the body knows before the brain does. That composure is a choice, not a trait. That the system holds when the person wavers — if there is a system.

I think about the cleaning company. Zero to 120 employees. The months where I didn't know if we'd make payroll. The partnership that worked until it didn't, and the dissolution that taught me more about leadership than any success I've ever had. I thought I was building a business. I was building a tolerance for ambiguity, a capacity for difficult decisions, and an identity that could hold loss without breaking.

I think about the mountains. The ultramarathon. The moments at altitude where the body said stop and something deeper said keep moving. I thought I was testing my limits. I was training execution discipline — the ability to follow through on a commitment when every system in my body was arguing for comfort.

I think about the betrayal in 2024. The season that demanded I still show up for my clients, my work, my integrity, under the full weight of something I hadn't chosen and couldn't control. I thought I was surviving it. I was learning to reframe at a depth I hadn't known was possible — to see the worst chapter of my life as the one that would make me a sharper, more honest, more compassionate coach.

And I think about now. This season. Caregiving for my wife. Caring for my mother. Building a practice and a body of work in the middle of a life that doesn't pause for ambition. Every morning, the same quiet question: *Who are you going to be today?*

Pressure was always the point.

Not the obstacle. Not the thing I had to push through to get to the good part. The pressure was the good part. It was the forge. It was the teacher. It was the mirror that showed me who I was and the fire that burned away everything I didn't need to carry.

Pressure was always the point. Not the obstacle. Not the thing I had to push through to get to the good part. The pressure was the good part.

I wrote this book because I believe you are in the middle of your own forge right now.

You picked it up because something in you recognized the pressure. The weight of decisions that affect people's livelihoods. The loneliness of leadership when the room is watching and no one is holding you. The gap between who you are under heat and who you know you're capable of being.

That gap is not a verdict. It's an invitation.

The system you've learned in these pages — Regulate, Reframe, Decide, Execute — is real. It works. Not because it's clever, but because it's built from pressure. From kitchen lines and partnership failures and mountain ridges and caregiving mornings and four decades of refusing to let pressure be the thing that defines me.

It's yours now.

Here's what I know after all of it.

The leaders who elevate under pressure aren't the ones who have less of it. They're not the ones with easier circumstances or better genes or thicker skin. They're the ones who made a decision — maybe the most important decision a leader can make — to stop fighting the pressure and start learning from it.

To stop performing under pressure and start being present inside it.

To stop asking *When will the pressure stop?* and start asking *Who am I becoming because of it?*

That question is the whole book. That question is the whole system. That question is the whole point.

The pressure isn't going to stop. You know that. If you're a leader, if you're building something, if you care about people and outcomes and doing work that matters — the pressure is the price of the life you've chosen. And it's a price worth paying.

Because on the other side of pressure — inside it, not beyond it — is the leader you were always meant to become.

Not someone else. Not a better version of someone else. You.

Regulated. Clear. Grounded. Present.

Leading.

The system is built.

The identity is clear.

Now go lead.

WHAT HAPPENS NEXT?

You've just finished *Elevate Under Pressure*™.

But this wasn't meant to stay on the page.

Because the real work doesn't happen in reading.
It happens in the moments where pressure hits—and you choose who you are.

If something in this book resonated with you, there's a reason.

You're not looking for more information.
You're ready for a different level of performance.

The question is simple:

What happens next?

Discover Your Pressure Profile

Every leader has a default under pressure.

Controller. Avoider. Reactor. Disconnector.

Most leaders never identify theirs—so they keep repeating it.

The Pressure Profile Assessment gives you a clear, immediate view of:

- How you default under pressure
- Which arenas trigger you most
- The hidden belief driving your response
- Where your leadership is costing you performance

This isn't a theory. It's a diagnostic.

Take the Pressure Profile Assessment:
elevateunderpressure.com/pressure-profile

(5–7 minutes. Immediate insight.)

Work With Scott Sadler

Scott Sadler is Leadership Performance Architect, ICF, Professional Certified Coach (PCC) and former Chief People Officer who helps leaders perform when it matters most.

His work centers on one outcome:

Helping leaders execute under pressure without losing clarity, composure, or trust.

Through the Pressure Performance System™, Scott works with:

- Senior leaders and executives
- Founders and growth-stage entrepreneurs
- Leadership teams navigating high-stakes change

His approach integrates:

- Identity clarity
- Emotional regulation
- Execution discipline

Because leadership isn't tested in calm conditions. It's revealed under pressure.

Ways to Work Together

Executive Coaching

For leaders operating in high-stakes environments who need to perform consistently under pressure.

Leadership Team Development

Align your leadership team to execute clearly, communicate effectively, and perform under pressure as a unit.

Keynotes & Workshops

Bring the Pressure Performance System™ into your organization through high-impact, actionable sessions.

Start the conversation:

www.elevateunderpressure.com and www.scottsadlercoaching.com

Or connect directly on LinkedIn

Pressure will never leave your life.

If you lead, if you build, if you care—it's part of the deal.

The difference is no longer whether you feel it.

The difference is who you become inside it.

You don't need less pressure.

You need a system.

Now you have one.

— Scott Sadler

ABOUT THE AUTHOR

Scott Sadler has spent four decades at the intersection of leadership, human performance, and pressure.

His path started in a kitchen. At sixteen, he stepped onto a high-end restaurant line and learned the foundational truth that would shape his entire career: pressure doesn't break people—it reveals them. That lesson followed him from restaurant kitchens to entrepreneurship, where he built and scaled a commercial cleaning company from zero to 120 employees and $1.2 million in revenue. It followed him through the dissolution of that business partnership—one of the defining leadership crucibles of his life. And it followed him into a 23-year executive coaching practice, where he has worked with hundreds of CEOs, C-suite executives, founders, senior leaders and managers navigating the highest-stakes moments of their careers.

From 2020 to 2025, Scott served as Chief People Officer for a growing credit union, where he experienced firsthand what it takes to build leadership culture from the inside—and what happens to organizations when leaders are misaligned under pressure. That experience deepened his conviction that the people side of leadership isn't a soft skill. It's the hardest skill. And it's where organizations either elevate or collapse.

Scott is an ICF-credentialed Professional Certified Coach (PCC), a Gallup Certified Strengths Coach, a Certified Executive Coach, Certified EQ-i 2.0 Practitioner, a Master Life Coach, and a Master Neuro Linguistic Practitioner (MNLP) and Certified Breath Coach.

His coaching integrates strengths-based development, emotional intelligence, and the neuroscience of performance under pressure into a practical system that leaders can use in the moments that matter most—not just in the seminar room, but in the boardroom, the difficult conversation, and the quarter where everything is on the line.

Outside of his coaching practice, Scott is a nature enthusiast who has tested his own relationship with pressure on mountain ridges, in ultramarathons, and in wilderness environments where performance isn't optional. He is a mountaineer, a backpacker, and a lifelong student of what it means to perform when the conditions demand everything you have. He is a daily meditator and yoga practitioner and still loves to run, golf and bike.

He is also a caregiver and a cancer survivor. In this season of his life, Scott is caring for his wife, who has advanced Alzheimer's. The pressure of caregiving is unlike any other—intimate, relentless, and invisible to most of the professional world. It is also the pressure that has most deeply refined the system in this book. The Pressure Performance System wasn't built in a classroom. It was built in a life that demands every tool it teaches.

Scott lives in Oregon. He works with leaders nationally.

---

scottsadlercoaching.com

elevateunderpressure.com

ACKNOWLEDGMENTS

This book was built under pressure. Which feels appropriate, given the subject.

It was also built with the support, patience, and belief of people who deserve to be named — because no system gets built alone, and no book gets written without the people who hold you steady while you're doing the work.

Family

My mother Norma, my father Jim, and my two younger brothers Shawn and Jason are my foundation. I am proud of all of them, and they are always there for me — no matter what. My grandparents, long since gone, were hugely influential in my life. The values they planted still hold.

To Ingrid, my wife of thirty years. Alzheimer's changed us in ways neither of us could have imagined. But your caring and kindness never wavered — nor did your support for me, even during the hardest moments. You are woven into every page of this book, whether you know it or not.

Clients

To the executives, founders, and leaders who trusted me with their pressure — you are this book. Every story, every framework, every tool was refined in the fire of your real leadership moments. I cannot name you here, but you know who you are. And you know what we built together.

A special thank you to Kevin Cole— the CEO who let me coach his teams and who gave me critical, honest feedback through every move in this system. That engagement made the book better.

Melissa Hedstrom

My co-facilitator in VitalEdge Wellness Coaching. Melissa's role in helping me deepen the somatic and wellness dimensions of my life and work cannot be overstated. Together we have built a wellness retreat practice (vitaledgewellnesscoaching.com) that has been enriching for our clients and for us — connecting and grounding in healthy, simple ways. Taking breaks from routine to explore the human experience through nature, body, mind, and spirit. This work feeds my soul.

Mentors and Colleagues

I have had so many mentors and coaches who shaped my thinking and supported me along the way that I could never name them all. Here are some of them — but please know I appreciate every one of them equally.

Chef Walter Hausermann. Chef Frank Sawyer. Doug Schmick. Chef Farrokh Larijani. Coach Jennifer Powers. Coach Drayton Boylston. Coach and colleague Jenna Forster. Coach Donna Stoneham. Colleague and mentor Robin Rose. Mentor Mike McLaran. Maps Credit Union President/CEO Mark Zook. And my first business mentor, who took pity on a clueless entrepreneur in 1989— Ron LeBlanc.

Each of you left a mark. The work I do today carries pieces of what I learned from you.

The Kitchen

To the cast of characters of chefs, cooks, servers, busboys, caterers, bartenders, and managers who taught a kid what pressure actually means — you gave me the foundation for everything in this book. You didn't know it then. I didn't know it then. But the kitchen was the first and most exciting classroom, the ticket rail was the first system, and the lesson was always the same: regulate first, or the line breaks.

The Mountains

I love all of nature, but the mountains will always hold a special place in my heart. They accepted me, tested me, and some of my greatest accomplishments happened up there — as well as some of my deepest spiritual experiences. My climbing partners over the years, and the bonds we built between us, are among my fondest memories.

A special nod to one of my closest friends, Mark. We accomplished much together (on the mountains and in life) and saw real danger, and yet here we are — still kicking. I wouldn't want to climb with anyone else.

And to another best friend — Jeff. You and I shared the pressure of the ultramarathon trail run, and it was one of the hardest things I have ever done in my life. I still regard the years of training with you as the best part of the experience — and the bonding through tough life moments we were able to share during the process meant more than any finish line.

The Reader

And to you — the leader who picked up this book because something in you recognized the pressure. Thank you for trusting me with your time and your attention. The system works. But it only works if you use it.

Pressure doesn't reveal weakness. It reveals identity. And now you have the system to choose what it reveals.

With gratitude,

Scott Sadler

Salem, Oregon — March 2026

www.ingramcontent.com/pod-product-compliance
Lightning Source LLC
LaVergne TN
LVHW010703110826
845149LV00014B/3218